DRIFT

"In a *dérive*, one or more persons during a certain period drop their relations, their work and leisure activities, and all their other usual motives for movement and action, and let themselves be drawn by the attractions of the terrain and the encounters they find there."
— Guy Debord, *Theory of the Dérive*, 1958.

The translation of *dérive* is *drift*.

PARIS

Photo by Bijan Sosnowski

06
Masthead

07
Welcome

158
Appendix

159
Glossary

08
Turkomania
Jonathan Shipley

12
Old and New, Side by Side
Ella McElroy

30
The Warp and Weft of Time
Eve Hill-Agnus

42
For the Love of Roasting
Sabrina Sucato

50
So Many Cafés
Paulina Paiz

56
A Cup of Coffee in Paris
J.R.M. Owens

66
Un Petit Cafe With a Side of Paris
Dale Arden Chong

74
À La Mode
Lane Nieset

88
Rencontre
Jae Lee

102
What We Eat With Coffee
J.R.M. Owens

114
Heartbroken in Paris
Laura Steiner

130
Flipping on the Lights
Maggie Spicer

136
Innovation Through Excavation
Jae Lee

142
The Roots of Café Chicorée
Shanthy Milne

146
Finding Love at Shakespeare and Company
Eve Hill-Agnus

152
A Winning Change
Anna Richards

ADAM GOLDBERG
Editor in Chief

DANIELA VELASCO
Creative Director

ELYSSA GOLDBERG
Editorial Director

BONJWING LEE
Executive Editor

CONTRIBUTORS
Anna Richards
Antúria Castilho Viotto
Augusta Sagnelli
Bijan Sosnowski
Carlotta Cardana
Clover Li
Dale Arden Chong
Ella McElroy
Eve Hill-Agnus
Fabian Schmid
Jae Lee
Jonathan Shipley
J.R.M. Owens
Julien Prebel
Karina Rikun
Lane Nieset
Laura Steiner
Maggie Spicer
Mickaël Bandassak
Paulina Paiz
Sabrina Sucato
Shanthy Milne
Sujin Kim
Tom Claisse

DEAR READER,

The late, great A.A. Gill—who I once spied, natty in tweed, across the dining room at l'Arpège—comically marveled at the foreign fascination with Paris in Vanity Fair:

"Why do they continue to come here? They can't all have brain tumors. The only rationally conceivable answer is: Paris. Paris has superpowers; Paris exerts a mercurial force field. This old city has such compelling cultural connotations and aesthetic pheromones, such a nostalgically beguiling cast list, that it defies judgment."

For decades, I shared Mr. Gill's bewilderment. From my earliest visits to Paris as a child, throughout college, when I spent summers there with my roommate's family, and well into my thirties, I remained unconquered by the city's fairy-tale charm. Globally celebrated and beloved, Paris always seemed excessively showy and syrupy to me, a cartoonish rendering of croissants and cliches for tourists and wilty dreamers.

And yet, Paris has remained my most frequent destination abroad. Having visited this ancient city dozens of times, I've been unable to escape its orbit. A capital of fashion, art, history, architecture, and romance, its offerings are undeniably manifold and irresistible. But sadly, aside from French staples like wine, cheese, bread, and pastries, I never considered reliably good food and drink—especially coffee—to be among them.

Thankfully, Paris has experienced a delicious awakening. In the past decade, the city's foodways have embraced a younger, more globalized generation, one that prizes diversity and quality in products, and is mindful of social impact. The result is a Paris with better cooking, better service, and better coffee.

In vol. 12 of Drift Magazine, our writers fan out across the twenty *arrondissements* that spiral like a giant snail shell from Paris's core along the Seine, and bring us stories of coffee that dovetail with the city's finest features. Eve Hill-Agnus peeks behind some of Paris's historic façades and finds reimagined spaces serving some of Paris's best roasts. Lane Nieset explores the overlap between fashion and the third wave. Jonathan Shipley takes us back centuries, when an Ottoman Turk arrived at Versailles with a magical bean that took the palace and Paris by storm. And everywhere, from an iconic bookstore on the Rive Gauche to Métro stations that dot the map, our writers tell of romance and heartbreak in the City of Light.

But lest you think we present a Paris transformed, Ella McElroy will quickly disabuse you of this notion. An expat hoping to open her own coffee shop, she's quick to point out the tension between the old and new, and hopes for a Paris where the tradition of cafes and brasseries can be preserved alongside an evolving coffee culture. And perhaps this is the key to understanding Paris's perennial appeal—it offers a magical *mélange* of memories and possibilities living side by side. It's not surprising that it has become an important intersection of life for so many, not the least of which is mine. Paris is, after all, where I first became acquainted with the publisher of this magazine, Adam Goldberg, over a decade ago.

Whether you are a lifelong admirer of this city, or like me, have slowly thawed to its allure, I hope the stories in the following pages will help you appreciate the many people and places that make Paris an exciting destination, not just for shopping and museums, but for drinking coffee.

BONJWING LEE,
EXECUTIVE EDITOR

Turkomania

WORDS
Jonathan Shipley

ILLUSTRATION
Clover Li

During the reign of Sultan Murad IV of the Ottoman Empire, drinking a cup of coffee was punishable by death.

It was a time during which religious leaders preached on the daytime street corners of Istanbul, warning passers-by that coffee inspired a litany of indecent behaviors. Those same streets found the sultan crusading against the beverage, eager to rout out coffee from his kingdom himself. He would disguise himself as a commoner and go down Istanbul's busy thoroughfares looking for those who were drinking the evil drink. If someone was found, the sultan would pull out his 100-pound broadsword and, there on the city streets, cut off the imbiber's head. Decaffeinated? More like decapitated, to be sure.

Murad IV's successor Ibrahim, who reigned from 1640 to 1648, was a little more lenient. The first offense earned a cudgel beating. If that person was caught drinking coffee a second time, they would be sewn into a sack and tossed into the Bosphorus River.

It wasn't until the ascendancy of Mehmed IV that coffee came into popular favor in the Ottoman Empire. Under Mehmed, coffee traveled to the far ends of the known world. As far, in fact, as the royal palaces of France.

Mehmed IV's emissary to France was Suleiman Aga. In 1669, Aga brought coffee to King Louis XIV at Versailles. Unfortunately, Aga was uncouth by French standards—presenting himself to the royal court in a simple wool coat, he refused to bow to the king. Angered, Louis XIV banished Aga from the palace to nearby Paris. However, the king kept some of those bags of coffee Aga brought, and found the drink delicious.

It wasn't just the Ottoman rulers of old who did not like coffee. Religious leaders of Europe didn't care much for it either, including those in France. Catholic church elders considered coffee to be an invention of Satan. Was the resistance against coffee stronger than the brew? The pope at the time would decide its fate. Pope Clement VIII, who had been the head of the Catholic church some years before Aga stepped foot at Versailles, was asked to damn the black, sooty beverage. He replied, "Let me taste it first." When he did, he is chronicled as saying, "This devil's drink is so delicious, we should cheat the devil by baptizing it." So, instead of condemning the drink, he embraced it. Clement VIII's papal endorsement went far for the beverage. Venice's first coffee house opened in 1645, and England's first followed shortly thereafter in 1650. Though coffee arrived in France ahead of Aga at the port of Marseille in 1644, it was Aga's banishment to Paris in 1669 that caused the beverage to take hold in the capital city and, subsequently, the rest of France.

Aga bedecked a house in Paris with Turkish tapestries and artwork, and infusing coffee with cloves, cinnamon, and sugar—sold by apothecaries as exotic ingredients—presented it to Parisians as a magical drink. He brewed coffee in elaborate contraptions, and had waiters in Ottoman garb serve it in fine china with napkins of embroidered muslin.

Parisians were charmed by this eccentric foreigner and his beguiling drink. The popularity of coffee skyrocketed. "Turkomania" swept the city, infecting courtiers, who made Ottoman etiquette for coffee consumption *à la mode*. Indeed, Ottoman culture as a whole made waves in Paris and beyond. Through Aga and his delegates, *Turquerie* took hold in all sorts of ways. The Orientalist fashion of the day, as well as decorative arts, music, painting, and more all have flavors of the land from which Aga traveled.

Here is an English account of Aga's triumph, written nearly two centuries later in 1851:

"If a Frenchman, in a similar case, to please the ladies, had presented to them his black and bitter liquor, he would be rendered forever ridiculous. But the beverage was served by a Turk—a gallant Turk—and this was sufficient enough to give it inestimable value… The eyes were seduced by the display of elegance and neatness that accompanied it; by those brilliant porcelain cups into which it was poured; by napkins with gold fringes, on which it was served to the ladies… add to this the furniture, the dresses, and the foreign customs… and you will allow that there was more than enough to turn the heads of French women."

Coffee drinkers were now turning heads rather than losing them. Small coffee shops began popping up throughout Paris, eager to emulate the gallant Turk's successes. These shops opened and closed with great rapidity. But one, which opened some years after Aga returned home, outlived its competitors. It is, in fact, still in operation and is not only the oldest coffee shop in Paris, but also the oldest operating coffee shop in the world.

A Sicilian chef named Francesco Procopio dei Coltelli had come to Paris around the year 1670. He had acquired a royal license to sell spices, ices, barley water, and lemonade. The savvy businessman added coffee to that list. It proved to be a wise decision.

It certainly helped his business, as did the Comedie-Française, a grand theater, which opened across the street from his establishment. The area quickly became a popular, cultural, and political gathering place. Notables began having coffee at the Sicilian's Cafe Procope. Voltaire was a regular—it is said that he drank dozens of cups of coffee a day, crediting the drink for helping him philosophize. Robespierre drank coffee at the cafe, as did Victor Hugo, Balzac, Oscar Wilde, Thomas Jefferson, Benjamin Franklin, Napoleon Bonaparte, Paul Verlaine, and Marie Antoinette.

After Aga's departure, Louis XIV grew his own coffee in the greenhouses at Versailles, as well as keeping a coffee tree in Paris's royal botanical gardens. By the time of Louis XV's reign, there were 600 cafes in Paris. And by the early 19th century, there were more than 3,000.

Today, Suleiman Aga's legacy can be found on most any Paris street corner. From the Champs-Élysées to Jardin des Tuileries, the 7th *arrondissement* to Montparnasse, the city now boasts approximately 7,000 cafes. From the Ottoman Empire Aga came, and with him, he brought the beginning of an empire of coffee.

—

Old and New, Side by Side

WORDS
Ella McElroy

PHOTOGRAPHS
Mickaël A. Bandassak

The emergence of the specialty coffee culture as we know it has progressed slowly in Paris. Third wave coffee shops and local specialty roasters, such as KB Coffee Roasters, Terres de Café, Belleville Brûlerie, and Coutume, appeared relatively late, beginning around 2010. This doesn't come as a surprise to many Parisians, particularly because the traditional French coffee psyche has been tied to a cultural staple for a century—the brasserie. Cue the image of bustling waiters on a terrace of woven rattan chairs, round bistro tables, and cigarette clouds trailing the air, all framing a *café crème* and a croissant. This is both a romanticized stereotype, and yet, quite accurate. The brasserie has been a symbol in French culture, and along with it, the typical "French-roasted" coffee. Generations of Parisians have accustomed their palates to its dark-roasted profile, and with the flowering of younger specialty coffee shops—which focus on carefully sourced, often single-origin beans that are roasted more lightly—the traditionally darker French coffee profile is being challenged. Between the nostalgia of the Parisian brasserie heritage and the growing international influence of specialty coffee, Paris is becoming a stage for the struggle between Old and New World coffee cultures.

Historically, the French palate is inclined to darker, sturdier, and typically more bitter coffee flavors, in part from its heavy consumption of chicory coffee during the Napoleonic era. Later, Robusta coffee, imported from French pre- and post-colonial states, replaced chicory, its darker roasted profile being similar to the flavor of chicory. The mass importation and production of Robusta coffee that followed throughout the World Wars ingrained its flavor profile in the French coffee culture. This economic and colonial model helped wean the French toward what most think of as the "French roast"—quite different from the more acidic, subtle, and lighter roast of an Arabica coffee found at specialty coffee shops today.

Many Parisians would get their coffee fix in a brasserie on their way to work, or during a quick break to fuel up. Coffee was often paired with a hard-boiled egg for a bit of protein, a tradition that can still be observed in many brasseries and cafes today. That's because the 3,100 brasseries in Paris mostly focus on food, not coffee, which is merely an accessory to the often expansive menu of classic dishes. Often opting for quantity rather than quality, brasseries mostly rely on large roasters that sell cheaper Robusta beans or blends. Because these roasters, like Cafés Richard, tend to be household names, the French are not only familiar with the taste and quality but also have a nostalgic connection to them.

Given the tendency for most Parisians to drink darker roasted espressos, the third wave coffee shop took time to establish itself in Paris. Finally, after over a decade, Paris now boasts a little over 100 of these types of coffee shops, dozens of which are uniquely dedicated to high-quality, specialty coffee. They've begun changing the coffee habits of younger and more globalized Parisians, while creating a recognizable space for expats and tourists, who are more accustomed to this kind of third wave experience.

Tourists tend to romanticize iconic brasseries like Café de Flore or Les Deux Magots, where famous writers and philosophers such as Simone de Beauvoire, Jean-Paul Sartre, and even Ernest Hemingway woke up and penned their thoughts around a cup of coffee. It offers a nostalgic and more "traditional" French experience, charmed with stereotypical *garçon* waiters, trimmed plants, and sidewalk tables on the buzzing streets. And yet, once they are checked off the list, more and more tourists head to Paris's specialty coffee shops, which offer a more familiar coffee culture.

As the French coffee market creates more space for this new type of coffee culture, it has also introduced a new form of

Dreamin' Man

Yuichiro Suguyama & Kaede Sato, Dreamin' Man

PARIS — 17

Nicolas Alary & Sarah Mouchot, Holybelly Café

20 — PARIS Kawa Coffee

Quentin Gauthier & Ludovic Fekete, La Main Noire

La Main Noire PARIS — 25

Marion Stephan, On Partage

On Partage

socialization to the French: brunch. Brunch has taken Paris by storm, and with it, the spread of higher quality coffee by local Parisian specialty roasters, like Fève Coffee and Kawa Coffee. Sundays have become popular at Café Mericourt or La Main Noire, each of which has introduced an Americanized and Aussiefied menu of pancakes, avocado toasts, carrot cakes, and granola bowls alongside specialty coffee drinks like flat whites, cold brews, and filters. Other coffee shops offering food, like Holybelly Café or On Partage, prefer to create original dishes based on locally sourced and seasonal French products.

While coffee shops like Boot Café (opened in 2013) and Téléscope Café (opened in 2012) helped set the scene of specialty coffee in Paris, they attracted foreigners and a small community of specialty coffee lovers in the city rather than local or French people. Most of these coffee shops were very small, making it financially and practically easier to survive. But gradually, the arrival and success of brunch-based coffee shops, which started incorporating third wave coffee products, like flat whites, V60s, aeropress, and single-origin espressos, helped introduce specialty coffee and roasters to a French audience. Through food, Parisians became acquainted with third wave coffee, enabling more specialty coffee shops to open. Like the earlier third wave shops, these newcomers, like Dreamin' Man, Hexagone Café, Motors Coffee, and Fringe Coffee Shop, also tend to source from international specialty roasters that focus on medium to light roasts, quality Arabica beans, more nuanced roasting profiles, transparency, and coffee origins, that attract the more conscious consumer emerging in Paris. While this kind of globalized coffee shop culture does not necessarily reflect French tradition, it is helping to dissolve language and cultural barriers by welcoming a more diverse clientele, including locals.

This has created a bit of a divide between different generations of Parisians in terms of coffee profile taste, social habits, and differences in price, value, and quality. At the same time, a new social movement for local, organic, ecological, and meaningful products and commerce has emerged in Paris, supporting smaller artisans and businesses that are typically backed by young, progressive, or globalized Parisians. Now more than ever, the city is welcoming independent coffee shops that highlight quality and transparency in their products and practices.

So, are coffee shops replacing brasseries? Not necessarily. Brasseries remain an institution of French culinary and social tradition. Many Parisians still enjoy the traditional French cafe culture they offer, and don't necessarily see French culture reflected in specialty coffee roasters, nor do they see their heritage reflected in a product that is unrelated to their land and *terroir* like their prized wine or cheese. While specialty coffee lovers may like to think that a coffee revolution has taken over Paris, the reality is that the majority of French and Parisian coffee drinkers still consume darker roasted coffees at home, or in brasseries and cafes. But, more than ever, specialty coffee shops now stand a better chance of existing alongside brasseries as an alternative option, providing a different type of relationship with coffee.

As an American in Paris with a Parisian partner, looking at things from the outside provides perspective and further highlights the cultural coffee battle while opening our coffee shop Clove. When explaining our concept to my French grandparents, products like drip coffee, cold brew, flat whites, and cookies seem familiar to me. In return, they lovingly correct our "misunderstanding" of French coffee culture and redirect us to their familiar espresso, *café crème*, croissants, and *pain au chocolat*. It is an eye-opening experience, putting into question whether financial models based on exclusively offering specialty coffee will work with Parisian habits. How do we respect the balance between French tradition and progressive Parisians; between people like my grandparents and international tourists? As we find a bridge between the two, while keeping our voice and values, we hope to help establish a new tradition alongside the classic brasserie culture in Paris—the coffee shop.

—

Café Kitsuné

The Warp and Weft of Time

WORDS
Eve Hill-Agnus

PHOTOGRAPHS
Antúria Castilho Viotto

Of all the Parisian emblems—the bicycle, the beret, the baguette—the vintage shop façade may be one of the most enduring, visible, and revered.

Its face reveals the heart of the city, which beats to the pulse of *les petits commerces*: small businesses—the bakers, butchers, and candlestick-makers. Strict building codes preserve these exteriors, some of which are classified as *monuments historiques* by the Ministry of Culture.

Today, some of these precious spaces are inhabited by coffee shops, with owners who embrace history and understand that it assigns them a role as stewards of important portals between the city's past, present, and future.

***

In the Palais Royal garden, a canopy of linden trees rustles in tidy rows and frames the entrance to a quaint Parisian coffee shop.

Café Kitsuné—it is one of several locations of a coffee shop born of international Franco-Japanese music and fashion label Maison Kitsuné, though the only one with a historic façade—sits under the surrounding arches, tucked into what was previously a luxury textile shop. Instead of tweed, the iconic offering is now a fox-shaped shortbread cookie (the fox is the brand's logo as well as its namesake in Japanese).

In sinuous script, the moniker "Jules Tournier et Fils" is spelled out above the windowpane. Before you enter the elegant, spare space for an iced matcha latte, toasted buckwheat tea, or affogato, look down: a threshold mosaic tells you the venerable 18th century horological titan Charles Oudin—who fashioned a timepiece for Empress Josephine and was also clockmaker for the French Navy—likewise hung his shingle here.

***

On the outside, an old shoe repair shop's painted storefront remains a faded, cerulean blue. Phillip Euell's tiny Boot Café, opened in 2014, boasts just enough room for six seats at round, marble-topped tables inside. Outside, the sidewalk offers a narrow ledge for a quick espresso, and a few stools when the weather permits.

Euell, a designer of Le Labo perfume boutiques, had driven by this little *cordonnerie* (cobbler shop) near rue Froissard in the Marais and yearned for a personal project. Moving from New York City in 2013, he had found very little specialty coffee in the City of Light at the time and decided to slip into the space and the business.

Boot Café features a rotating roast from veteran roaster Fuglen in Oslo, Norway. When it first opened, there were no alternative milks on the menu, and Euell and his wife, who works in the fashion industry, rose at 5 a.m. to bake scones, chocolate chip cookies, and olive oil cakes at home, while their kids slumbered. Now another couple—expats from San Francisco—drops off pastries daily to the barely nine-square-meter shop. Within, you feel both bohemian and well-heeled, and imagine the life this shoebox had before.

***

At Café Nuances, in the 1st *arrondissement*, near the chic Place Vendôme, the city's center of money and luxury. Behind the marble, Art Deco-era façade that reads "*laiterie, beurre, oeufs*" (dairy, butter, eggs), awaits a coffee bar with boldly futuristic lines. This was the dream for 23-year-old Charles Corrot, who joined with the trendy design firm Uchronia in 2021 and turned this former creamery—listed a *monument historique*, it has appeared in films—into a timeless capsule.

The cafe's original mosaic floor and glass-tiled ceiling, which features an Art Deco star design, have been restored (hidden by the previous tenant, a hairdresser). But everything else inside is an unexpected time warp. Ultra-modern, illuminated resin shelves in violet, yellow, and chartreuse shingle back, drawing your eye to the cafe's centerpiece—a dazzling, avant-garde coffee bar. Like a Space Age fantasy, the steel counter, set against a bright-orange wall, is a spotlit stage upon which the third wave is showcased. Although Corrot's designs strike a bold contrast, juxtaposing the past with the future, the nuance here is found in the refined, specialty coffee. Baristas serve five coffees roasted in Paris, chosen for their range (aromas from tobacco to hazelnut and lemon).

32 — PARIS

36 — PARIS   Boot Café

CORDONNERIE

Café Nuances

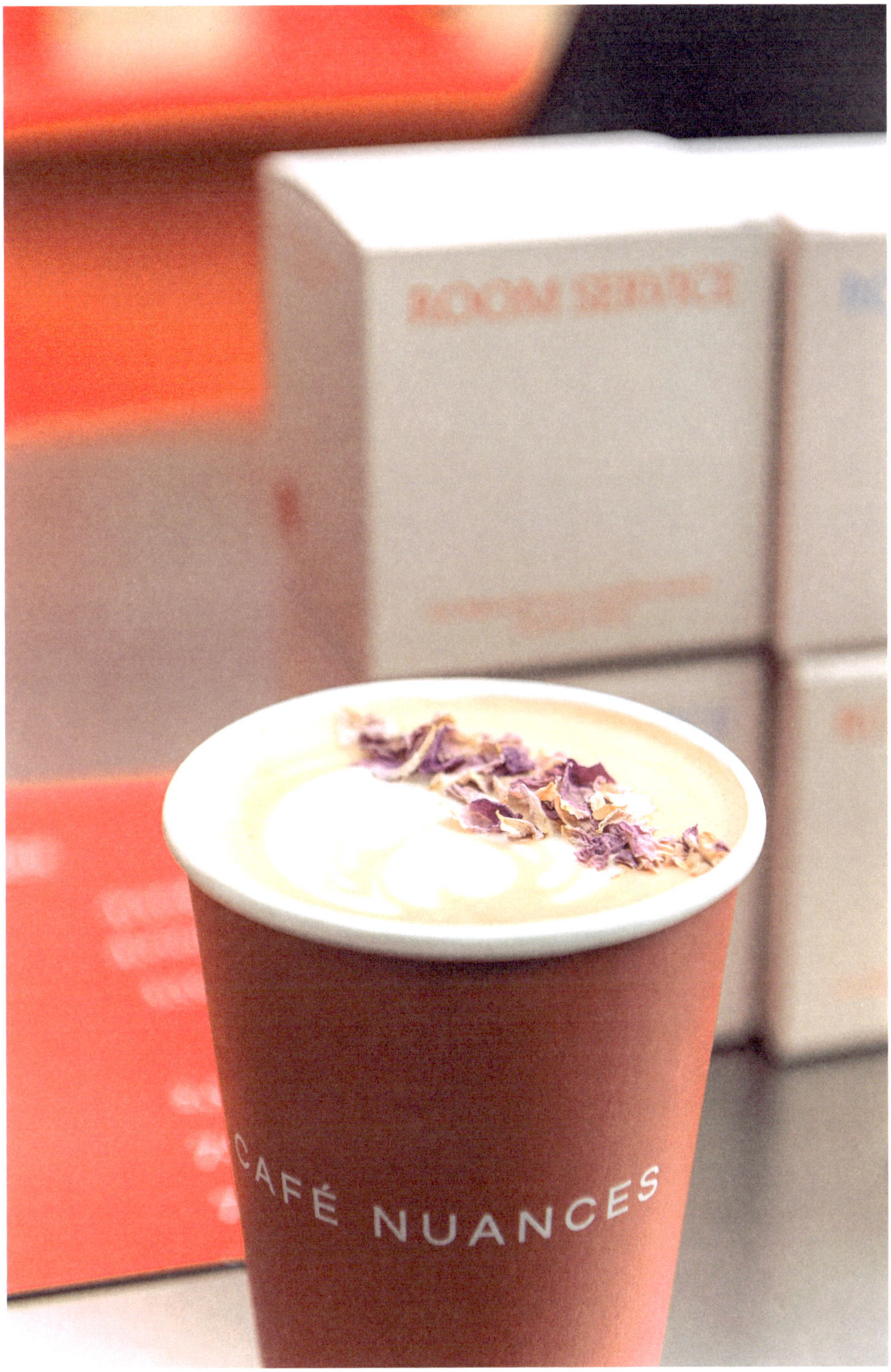
CAFÉ NUANCES

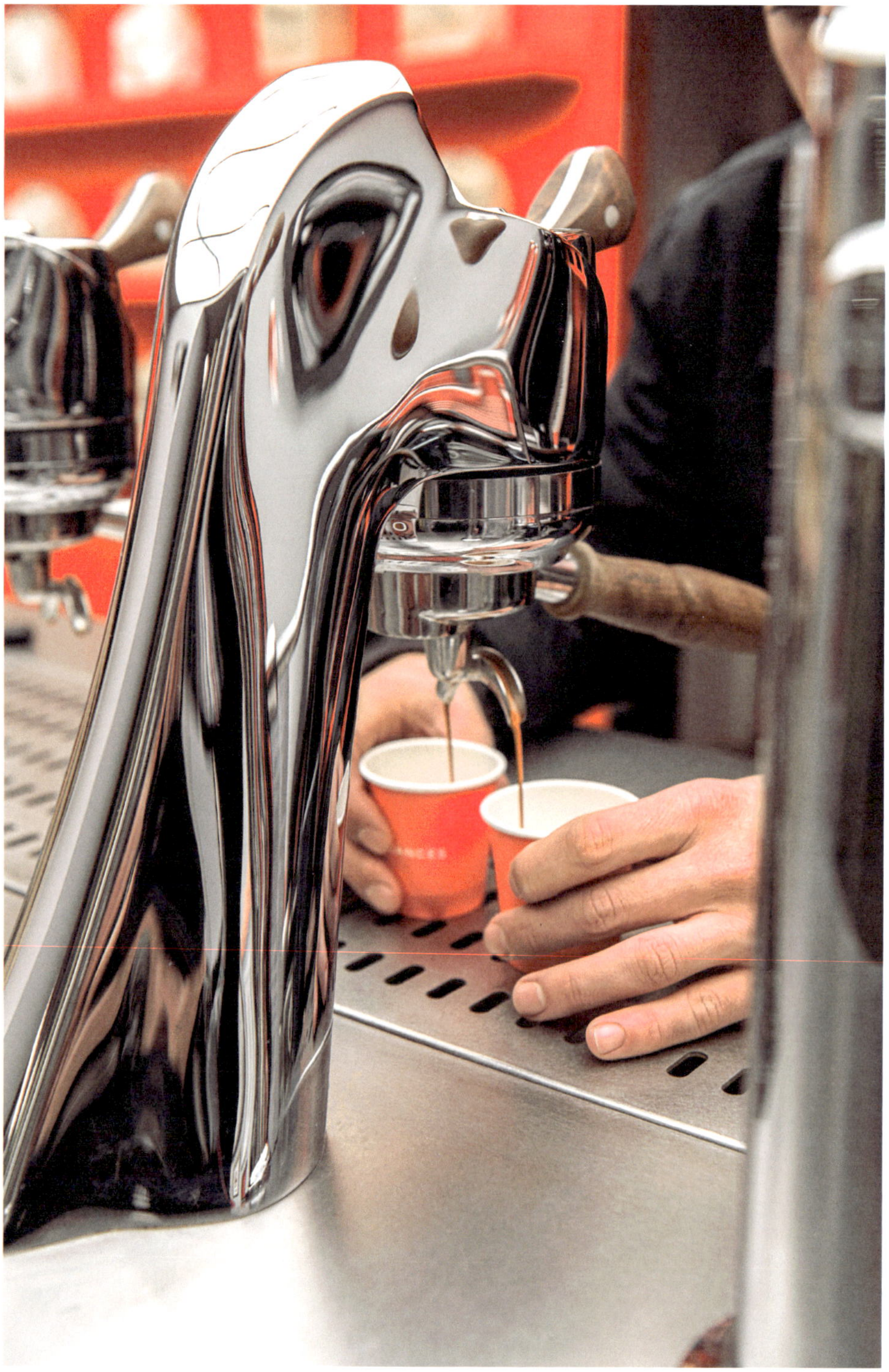

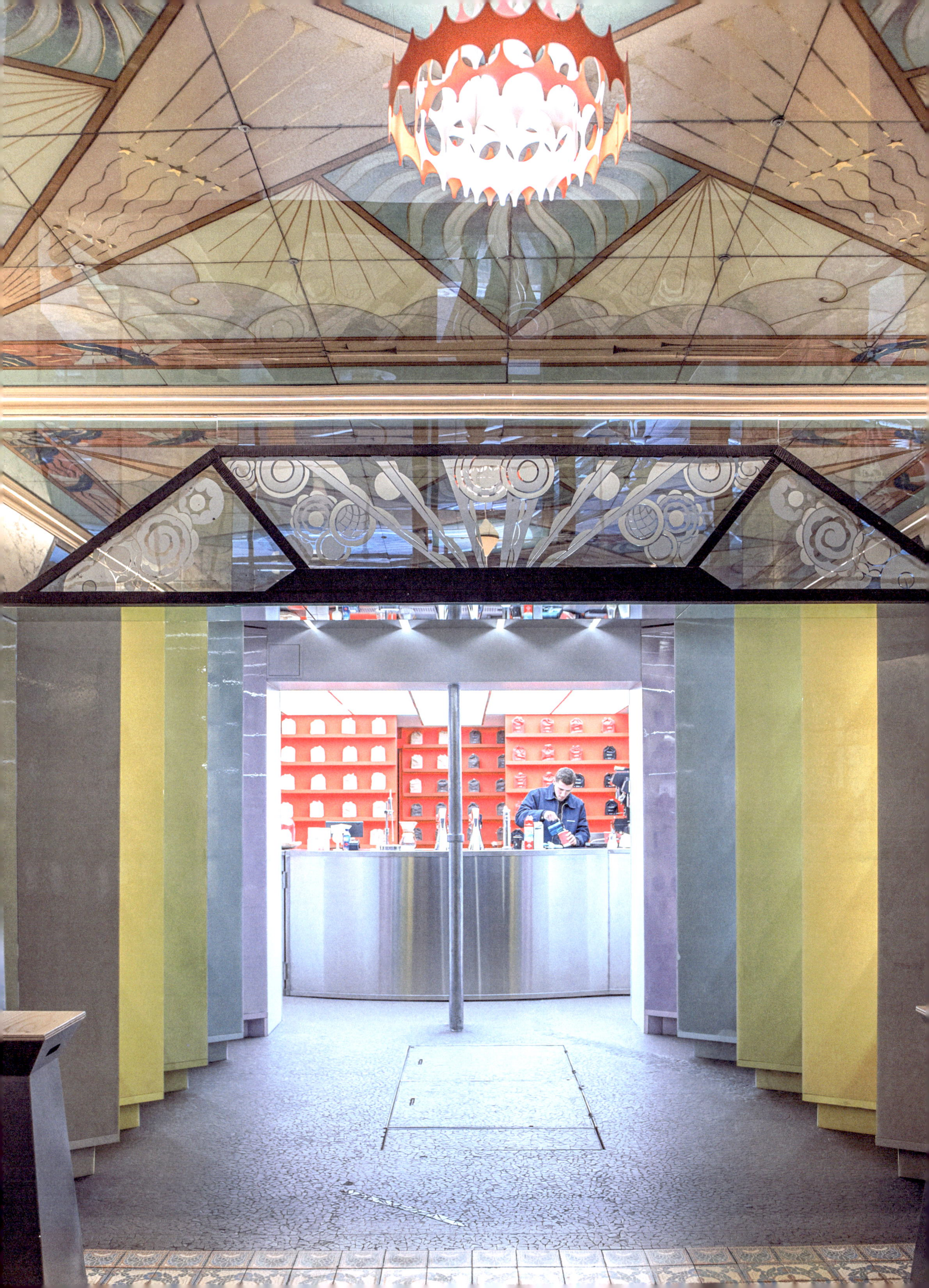

For the Love of Roasting

WORDS
Sabrina Sucato

PHOTOGRAPHS
Carlotta Cardana

For roasters in Paris, it's all about the slow burn.

In a city that's over 2,000 years old, the fact that its coffee culture is a gradually developing phenomenon is hardly surprising. This is the land of finely aged wine and cheese, after all. Time isn't just a measure of what makes the city's food and drink exceptional; it's an *ingredient*.

Because of this, the roasters seeking to introduce the wonderful world of coffee to the people of Paris understand that they have their work cut out for them. Sure, some of them may have started their businesses more than a decade ago. Even so, they know that, for Parisians, coffee isn't a love at first sight sort of deal. But, when done right, it's a relationship that can stand the test of time.

Take Coutume for instance—founded in 2010 on rue Babillon in the 7th *arrondissement*, Coutume is one of the earliest third wave roasters to leave its mark on Paris. Its arrival, along with that of a few other roasters during the time, marks the budding of the city's specialty coffee roasting scene, much of which dates back to the founding of the roastery La Caféothèque or, as it was known then, Solunas Cafés in 2005. Today, La Caféothèque, which has since transformed from a quaint cafe and roastery into a full-fledged roasting company with a top-tier barista and roaster training program, shares the city with a handful of talented roasters such as Coutume, which recognize the beautiful potential of great coffee for Parisians.

"It was a fully immersive experience with a roaster right in the back of the shop," recalls Tom Clark, one of Coutume's co-founders, of the cafe's early days. "We had Arabica coffee plants growing in sinks."

For Clark, an Australian who fell for the city during a university exchange, Paris was the ideal place to develop a coffee culture,

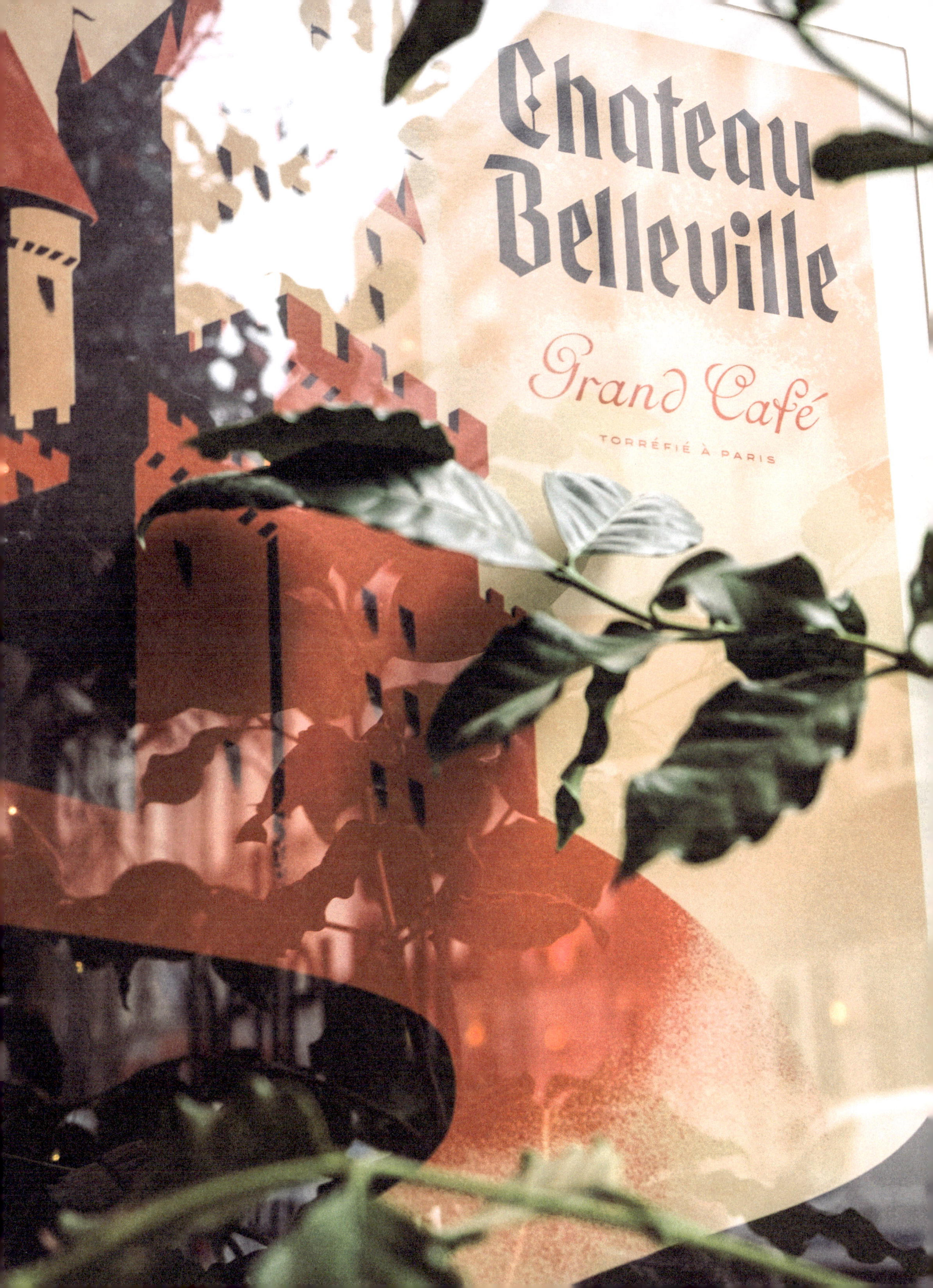
Chateau
Belleville
Grand Café
TORRÉFIÉ À PARIS

Mihaela Iordache, Belleville Brûlerie

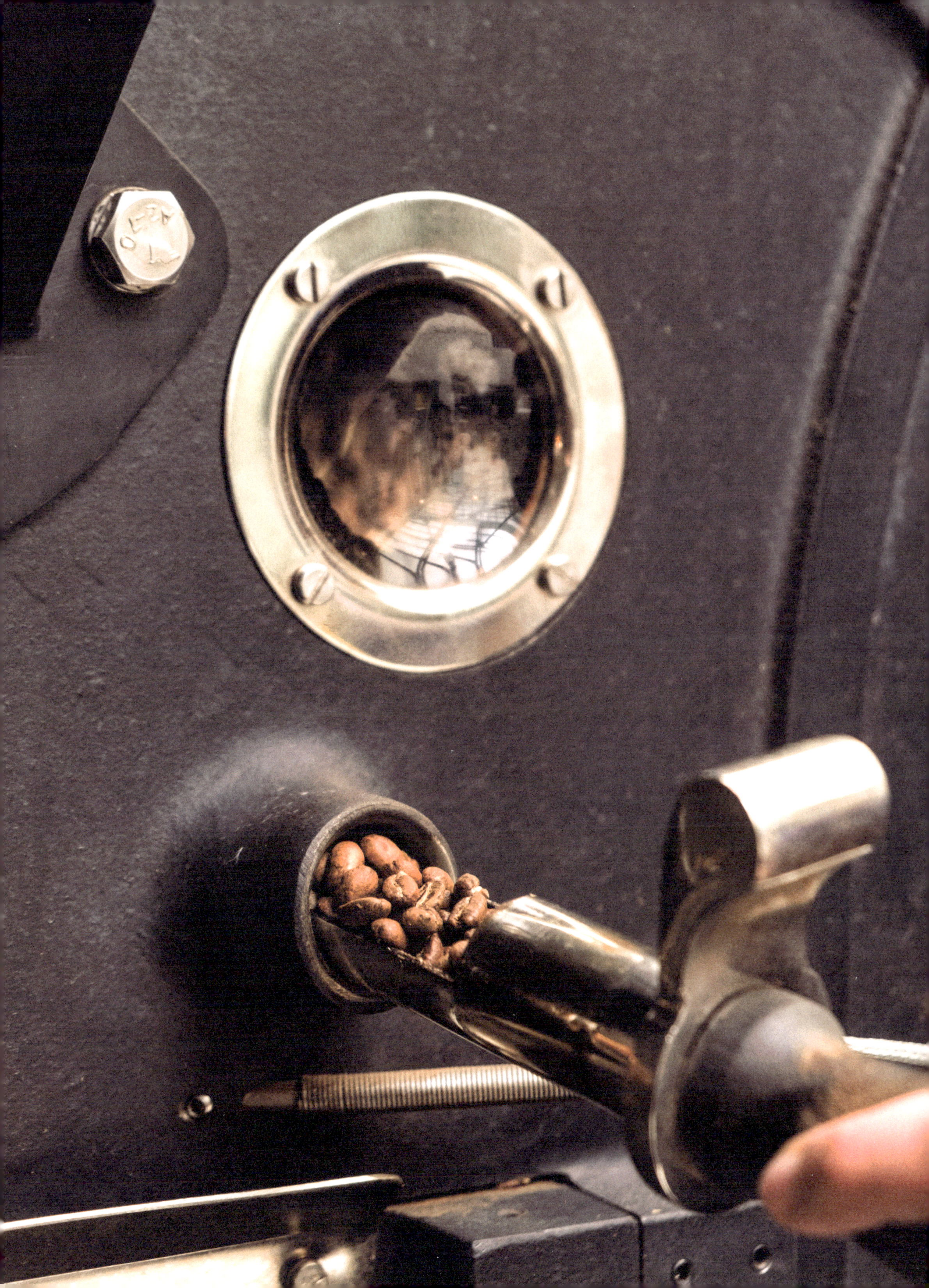

David Nigel Flynn, Belleville Brûlerie

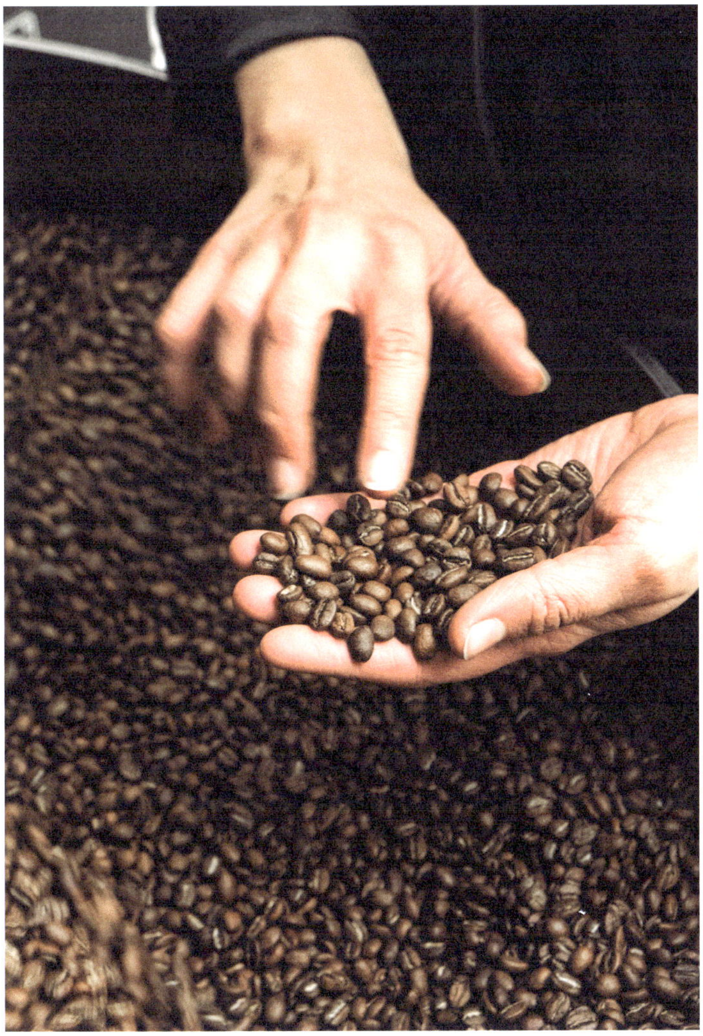

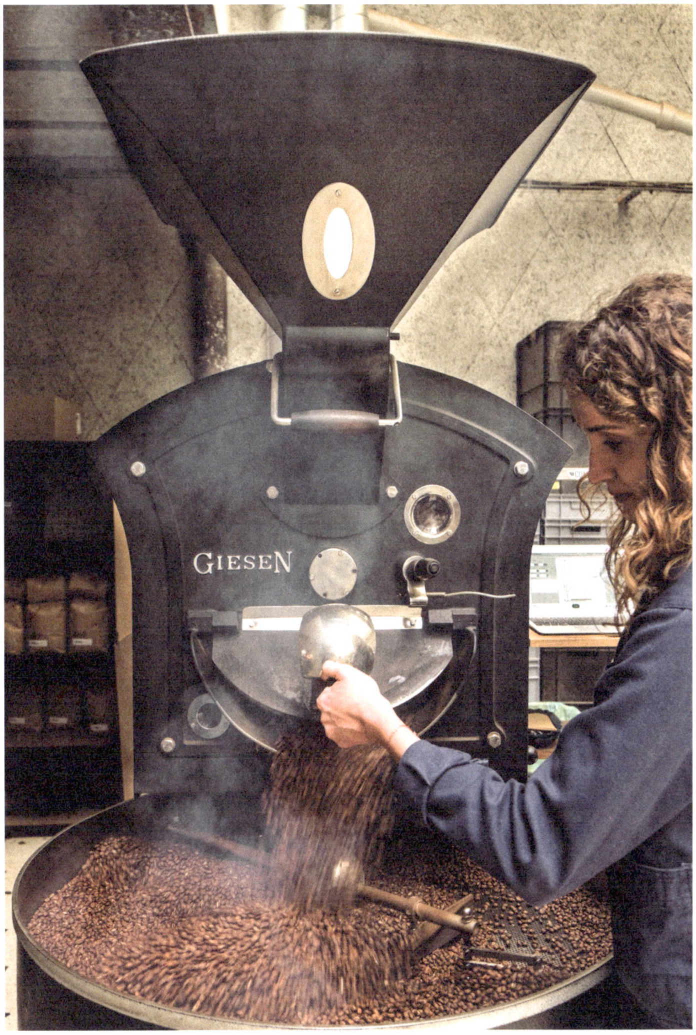
GIESEN

Tim Clark, Coutume

mostly because it was virtually nonexistent at the time. Over the years, he and his team grew their brand as they moved the roastery to a larger space in the 10th *arrondissement* and even took over as the coffee shop in the Galeries Lafayette, an upscale shopping center, during the pandemic, thereby replacing Starbucks with a distinctly Parisian brand.

"We're actively trying to grow the coffee community as a whole," Clark explains. For Coutume, which focuses on single-origin roasts, it's all about revealing the identities and stories behind the beans. "We elevate the personality of every coffee," he adds. Currently, Coutume's roasts are available both at its cafes and through its website, as well as through wholesale clients, which represent approximately 50% of the brand's business. Coutume takes a hands-on approach with clients, spending 10 hours working with them and educating them on proper roasting techniques.

"The more we invest our passion and energy, the more demanding we become," Clark notes. "We're always on the forefront and looking to improve."

Like Coutume, Lomi was another early entrant to the Parisian roasting scene. Founded in 2010, Lomi was born from a desire to tap into the city's potential and to deliver an unforgettable cup of specialty coffee. The brand, which focuses on wholesale relationships, got its start with a 3kg electric roaster in the 17th *arrondissement* before eventually relocating to a cafe and roasting space in the 18th *arrondissement*.

"Looking back it was a bit crazy and lucky we were located on a quiet street, otherwise the smoke we were sending out the front door might have been a problem," recall co-founders Aleaume Paturle and Paul Arnephy. Their brand focus on three product categories: Les Parcelles, a series devoted to producers with which Lomi has a longstanding relationship; Les Éphémères, a series of limited edition coffees; and J'ai Deux Amours, a signature blend that tastefully balances chocolate and fruit flavors.

Above all, Lomi seeks to sway the hearts of Parisians and tap into the potential the city has to offer.

"French culture demands that each idea needs to prove itself before being granted acceptance," Arnephy and Paturle observe. "The potential for real quality in France is really exciting."

That journey toward quality coffee resonates at KB Coffee Roasters, the Parisian roastery behind the KB Cafeshop and Back in Black cafes. For founder Nicolas Piégay, the idea for the brand came around 2008 when he envisioned not just a coffee shop in Paris, but also a space for "crafting good coffee, which turned out to be significantly more work than simply buying good beans." In 2010, he launched KB Coffee Roasters, which focused on seasonal, freshly harvested, and single origin coffees selected through extensive blind cuppings.

While KB Coffee Roasters is known for its two cafes, the brand also supplies around 30 spots throughout the city, as well as clients beyond France, thanks to its online presence. After initially roasting at The Beans on Fire, a roasting collective in the city, the company transitioned to roasting on its own, with a trusty Diedrich IR-12 machine powering the process. Piégay, along with head of the roastery Rémi Bompart and roaster Connor Bramley, work to craft coffees that make people stop and savor.

"Since we're fans of intense flavors, we usually have a good selection of naturally processed coffees with funky profiles and original tasting notes," the trio explains.

Just as making a statement is crucial for the roasters of Paris, so too is finding a way into the hearts—and palates—of Parisians. Fortunately, that's what Belleville co-founder and president David Nigel Flynn is all about. An expat from the United States, Flynn established himself in the city's budding coffee scene when he helped to found Télescope, a popular cafe in the 1st *arrondissement*. Yet, when he realized there was a lack of roasteries in Paris, he launched Belleville in 2015 to "reframe what French coffee could be."

"We felt like there was a really big gap for roasters that were quality driven and very French," he explains. To help with this, he and his team focused on six core blends, with rotating seasonal blends, in order to draw upon the tradition of blending in French spirits and wines. If Belleville's popularity in Paris is any indication, then Flynn's approach seems to be working. The company maintains a direct-to-consumer approach via boutiques in the city, as well as a strong online presence. Through both in-store interactions and online transactions, it promotes a connection with clients above all.

"One of the most important things we did was opening the roastery doors on weekends and the boutique every day," Flynn observes. "We have conversations with guests and interact with them. I think that had a really big effect."

Belleville isn't the only roaster to take a community-centric approach. For Saul Súaza of Wekoffee, making coffee readily available is essential. Súaza, a graphic designer by trade, co-founded the brand with his sister in 2014, having come from a family of coffee roasters in Colombia. In 2019, when the opportunity to move to France presented itself, he made the leap and began importing beans in small batches to expand Wekoffee's presence in Paris.

When choosing farms to work with, Súaza looks for three things: the story, the flavor, and the environment. Many of his beans come from Colombia, and he roasts them at The Beans on Fire, the same place where KB Coffee Roasters got its start.

For Súaza, the brand's mission is democratizing coffee. "Every person deserves good coffee and every farmer deserves good payment," he enthuses. While the brand makes approximately 60 percent of its sales online, the rest of its income comes from local businesses and restaurants. Wekoffee has a strong presence in *épiceries*, small grocery markets in France that are hubs for shopping and socializing among locals. He believes that if good coffee is at the store and easily recognizable, there's a greater likelihood that Parisians will notice it and buy it. And that's ultimately Súaza's goal: "We imagine coffee everywhere in a good way."

—

So Many Cafés

WORDS
Paulina Paiz

PHOTOGRAPHS
Fabian Schmid

We only had a weekend in Paris, but instead of a full itinerary I wanted to take in the city the way my mom and grandma had done before me: sitting at sidewalk cafes. Hoping my countless hours of listening to the podcast "Coffee Break French" would finally be useful, I took my Greek friend for a cultural immersion. He warned me that he had not heard great things about French coffee, or service for that matter. I did not care—as long as I got to experience the French equivalent of a coffee break: the *pause-café*.

After sitting down at a charming cafe in St-Germain, we saw the lady sitting at the table next to us dip her croissant in her coffee. In all honesty we were both a little bit appalled. Even though I know it is delicious, back home in Guatemala, doing this is considered bad manners. Later, when I looked this up, I read that this indulgence is customary for breakfast, or *le petit déjeuner*, and is usually accompanied by a *café au lait* or a *café crème*. And no, the latter does not have whipped cream. They are both strong coffee or espresso drinks with a bit of hot or steamed milk added. The main difference between the two is where you enjoy them: a *café au lait* is typically taken at home or at a hotel whereas a *café crème* is what you would order at a bar or at a cafe, and is usually only taken in the morning. Unlike other cultures, the French do not customarily have coffee drinks with meals after breakfast. Sometimes, people with a sweet tooth will order coffee at the end of a meal—a *café gourmande*, which is usually accompanied by three or four *mignardises* (mini-desserts).

My friend could not decide what to order, and the menu was not very helpful. I attempted to decode French coffee terms for him. Almost like a pH scale, French coffee drinks are generally distinguished by the strength of the coffee, determined mostly by how much water is added. A *café*, which is actually just espresso, not brewed or drip coffee, is the most popular order, and locals usually drink it during work breaks. Those wanting something less caffeinated will order *un déca*—short for *café décafeiné*. Un *café serré*, or simply, un *serré*, has almost half the water content as a full espresso. The word *serre* ("tight") is also used in the expression *serre-moi fort* which means "hold me tight," but in the context of coffee, *serre* refers to the amount of pressure put on the barista machine. At the other end of the spectrum is a *café allongé*, which literally translates to "elongated coffee," as the espresso is stretched by adding hot water.

Then there are coffee drinks with dairy or dairy alternatives added, like *café au lait* or *café crème*. My personal favorite is the *noisette*. It is the French version of a macchiato. Although I wish it had notes of hazelnut (*noisette* is French for hazelnut), the name actually refers to the color produced by adding a splash of milk or cream to espresso. Small details like these give you a window into how the French love to play with the language of coffee. For example, I find it amusing that they often remark: *"C'est (un peu) fort de café!"* ("The coffee is a bit strong!") when referring to something that is over the top or hard to believe.

The French lexicon for coffee might seem difficult to adopt at first, but as the owner of Café Loustic puts it, "The French don't like to dumb things down." One of the allures of Parisian cafes is the ability to people-watch on the terrace and get updated with the latest fashion trends. This is especially true in neighborhoods like Le Marais. But what makes these spots so unique is that the stylish crowds can co-exist with the intellectual ones, and it has historically been so.

In 1721, Baron de Montesquieu, who is credited for the theory behind the separation of powers in government, wrote that

SAINT PEARL

Saint Pearl

Typica

Left: Strada Café. Right: Café Loustic

"Parisians liked to go to cafes to play chess or to hear the latest news." Nowadays it is still possible to see people pondering their next move on a chess board, or reading a novel (and truly reading it) at a cafe. And cafes still host philosophical conversations between friends, as well as silent ones inside the minds of individuals who only have their ideas as company. If one would like to participate in cafe culture in Paris, it is not enough to study its vocabulary: one must also engage with its rigorous thinking. So it is no wonder that the baron ascribed almost magical qualities to French coffee—saying anyone who drank it would become "witty."

It is hard to find the balance between vibrant conversation and a serene thinking space, but many Parisian cafes have mastered this art, becoming a sanctuary for creatives and intellectuals alike. In his memoir of Paris "A Moveable Feast," Ernest Hemingway observed that "the French have a way of life into which all needs easily fit, as they have cafes where a young fellow can sit for hours over a *café crème*." A common misconception is that people spend this time simply relaxing. There are corners of Paris that still bear witness to political exchanges and the conception of future masterpieces. The cafes themselves have been the focus of great literary works and there are tours of the city dedicated to them. But nothing compares to the interactive opportunity of actually becoming fluent in the phrases, dynamics, and etiquette of the living cultural artifact that is the French cafe today.

As the waiter came over to take our order, I told my friend to greet him with "*bonjour*." I had read a review of Strada Café that said "waiters are now accustomed to (and [have] patience with) Americans who can't be bothered to learn some basic French words when vacationing in well… France." I am always surprised at how many tourists forget this courtesy, or even worse, consciously choose not to use it despite being familiar with the language. Even if it is the only French word you know and butcher its pronunciation, most Parisians will appreciate the gesture, if not expect it. Outside of France as well: when I notice the waiter is French and I ask for the bill saying "*l'addition s'il vous plaît*" I receive a genuine smile in return. They know their language is beautiful, and showing you appreciate it might just get you the service you want.

I must not have been great company to my friend that weekend. We sat in cafes for hours; I drank my coffee in silence, with every sip taking in the spoken and unspoken things being said around us.
—

Télescope

A Cup of Coffee in Paris

WORDS
J.R.M. Owens

PHOTOGRAPHS
Mickaël A. Bandassak

Twelve years ago, Oliver Strand announced in The New York Times that coffee in Paris "sucks so bad," which was true but missed the point. The reason the culinary capital of the world has been so hesitant to embrace the third wave of specialty coffee is that Parisians and third wave coffee culture view the drink in different ways. Paris's coffee culture is rooted in a time when French was the *lingua franca*, and this has complicated its introduction to specialty coffee, which has largely been influenced by the English-speaking world. The path forward for a Parisian expression of specialty coffee is not to rebuild Brooklyn by the Seine; the two are going to have to come to terms with each other if they are to coexist.

"What would Paris be without its cafes?" Anna Brones and Jeff Hargrove ask on the first page of their landmark 2015 survey "Paris Coffee Revolution." Conversations about coffee in Paris begin with its cafes, which is telling because the French cafe is not a coffee shop; it is not even a place for coffee. Since Le Procope opened in 1686, cafes have grown up with Paris and served its people as a daily place for visiting with friends or reading the newspaper while enjoying food or drink.

Cafes are not *for* coffee, any more than they are for Coca-Cola or cabernet. In the Parisian view, they are "a place you go and sit," says Nicolas Clerc, founder of Télescope Café in the 1st *arrondissement*. "Your purpose is to try to convince this girl or this guy to go with you, to try to seal this deal in a business, or to see your friend you haven't seen in a while. So this is the purpose of a coffee in France."

If Strand's 2010 verdict about coffee had been read aloud in the streets at that time, it might have been met more with disinterest than disgust: "Any French person will tell you [that the coffee in France] is bad," says David Flynn, co-founder of Belleville Brûlerie in the 19th *arrondissement*. "No one is under any sort of illusion it is good." Surprise at the sorry state of coffee assumes the point of coffee in Paris is quality. It is not. Clerc says, "Parisians can't care less about coffee—they love to have a nice place, they love to have a chat—but it's not a French thing." Coffee is not the point, community is.

With a preponderance of influence from the United States and Australia, the latest wave of coffee has been largely a New World phenomenon, from its early trailblazers to today's tastemakers. And its focus on quality confused the Parisian palate. "In France we are very slow to change things," says Chung-Leng Tran, co-founder of Hexagone Café in the 14th *arrondissement*. "We are too sure about our strength, and we had a strong coffee culture but it wasn't focused on quality."

***

"It's like a new world started to grow in Paris."
— Chung-Leng Tran

Into France's entrenched coffee culture, specialty coffee arrived in the early 2010s, bringing with it a distinctly foreign accent. "A lot of the cafes and roasteries that were opening up were very explicitly inspired by elsewhere," says Flynn, an American who moved to Paris in 2009. "The menus were in English. They weren't trying to be French—it was explicitly about not being French." Since there were no local, Parisian specialty coffee shops, it had to be imported largely by foreigners, who introduced a new type of establishment. Focused on the quality of the coffee, these coffee shops were distinctly different from

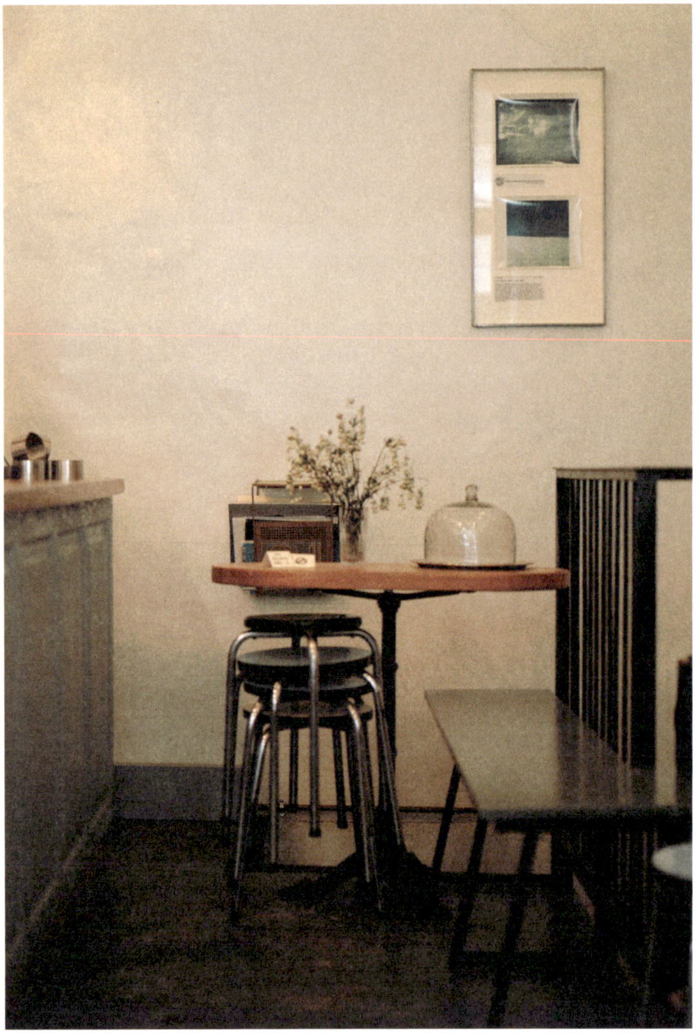

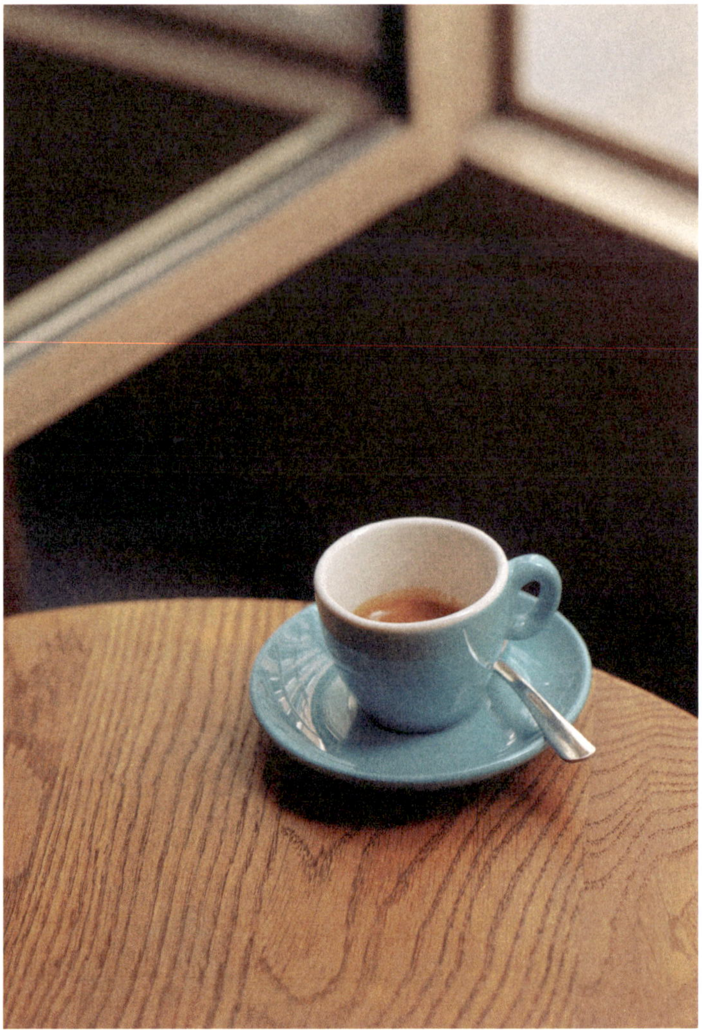

Télescope

Nicolas Clerc, Télescope

Parisian cafes and brasseries. Clerc, a Frenchman who trained in New York City at Blue Bottle and Intelligentsia, says, "The Australians, Americans, and Scandinavians sent specialty coffee to Paris, the places opened, and those places are filled with Australians, Americans, and Scandinavians."

Due in part to the high upfront cost of the *fonds de commerce* requisite for taking over a cafe space, expats and French people inspired abroad began opening in smaller, alternative locations throughout central Paris. "Specialty coffee kind of got tied to this notion of coffee shop, for better and for worse," Flynn says. While coffee shops were novel and trendy, as a concept they are "not very well suited to the culture"—a culture shaped by and at Paris's traditional cafes. The coffee shop, as a small space reliant on carry-out, is a "business model [that] doesn't really work that well in France," he says, because "French people don't get coffee to go, period."

Clientele were "hip French people that traveled abroad, and tourists," Flynn says. "And that was the case for a lot of the coffee shops well into the middle of the 2010s." So, although specialty coffee grew in Paris, it did so in a distinctly non-Parisian way. "In France we cannot use the term 'third wave,'" says Tran, who has lived in Paris since infancy. "I think 'third wave' is something specific to the U.S." If the second wave was defined by Starbucks (and similar chain coffee shops)—distinguishing it from what existed before as the first wave, and what followed as the third—then the typology doesn't work in a place like France, where Starbucks never typified a wave. "In France, you didn't have that kind of evolution. It's a different history."

***

"Specialty coffee and coffee shops are not necessarily one and the same. You can have specialty coffee outside of the coffee shop."
— David Flynn

The financial reality of Paris forced specialty coffee to reimagine itself in Parisian terms. The coffee shops that sprung up throughout Paris faced high rents and employee taxes, and those that lasted were soon forced to venture beyond their carry-out dependent model: hence food-focused shops like Holybelly and roasters like Belleville Brûlerie.

The *brûlerie* was a neighborhood staple in postwar France, roasting and selling coffee to locals. Literally "burner," the word *brûlerie* provides insight into the historic French palate set centuries ago by bitter-tasting robusta beans from colonial West Africa. Flynn created Belleville Brûlerie to introduce specialty coffee to Parisians in a form with which they felt comfortable. The *brûlerie* and its boutique retail outlet "[work] very well in a French culture where you'll go to the baker for your bread, the vegetable shop for your vegetables, the butcher for your meat, and the coffee roaster for your coffee."

Belleville's boutique gives Flynn a forum in which to address one of the key hurdles facing specialty coffee anywhere in the world: education. "We have amazing conversations about coffee with clients in our boutique," he says, "conversations that would make any barista anywhere else in the world jealous."

Coffee shops are busy places full of noise, not meant for talking over the counter about M.A.S.L. (meters above sea level) and extraction. At Télescope, Clerc says the goal is to serve good coffee without bothering the client about why it's good. "You

David Nigel Flynn, Belleville Brûlerie

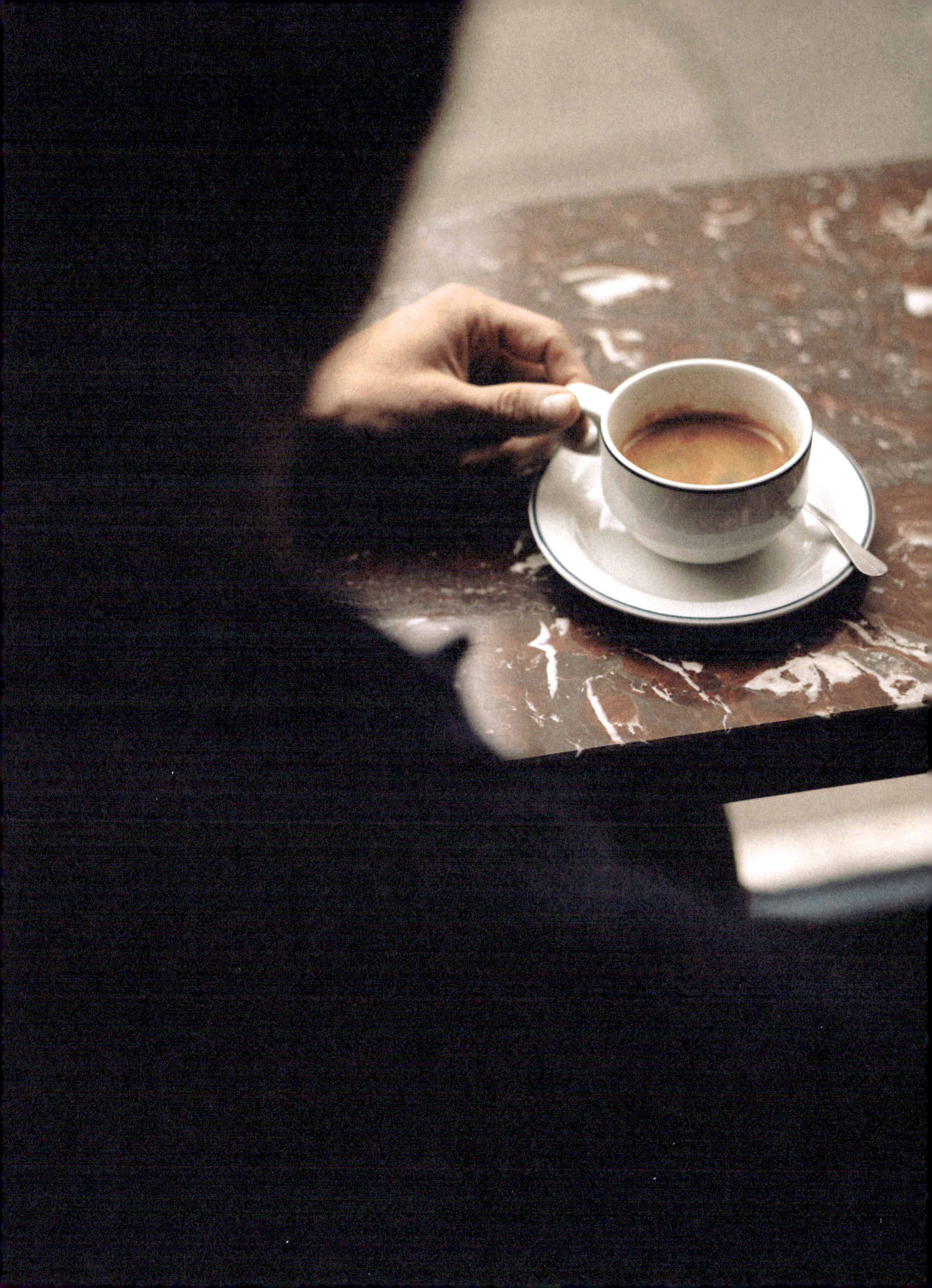

go, 'You want a coffee? Here it is.' And then we can talk about everything they want. If they have questions about coffee, I am the happiest to answer, but we will never bother them with it." Tran agrees: "You don't want to be coffee snobs…We want to roast the coffee perfectly, we want to perfectly brew the coffee—but we don't want to be picky with people."

For Flynn, a coffee shop is "not a good format for conversation or teaching people things. It's just not really what it's for. But a boutique can be." And in France where "thinking something should cost more because it tastes good is so obvious it doesn't even bear mentioning," the culture, he says, is "a really fertile environment for talking about [specialty coffee], if you can get yourself in a situation to talk about it."

Now, more than a decade into the city's coffee revolution, "there [are] a lot of different faces of specialty [coffee] within Paris, and growing," he says, citing restaurant-style places, coffee shops, boutiques, and traditional cafes serving quality coffee. Through Belleville, he says, "We really wanted to decouple specialty coffee and coffee shops in Paris."

***

> *"Coffee is exactly as cool as skateboarding—as complicated, as demanding, and as cool."*
> —Nicolas Clerc

In the days when coffee in Paris sucked, Tran was surfing the internet for blogs and videos to learn how to brew at home. "I started like that, from zero, to try to make coffee myself."

About that time Flynn started Frog Fight, a gathering of coffee-loving people in Paris. He said he'd do it if 10 people committed. The first night, 30 came. "Those Frog Fights were probably the first time there was an event in Paris that you could go to and learn about specialty coffee without having traveled abroad," he says. Soon, Tran was coming. "I started to meet people," Tran says. "I started to love coffee and the community. I found that the people in the coffee community [were] very friendly, very kind. I wanted to be a part of it."

"Back in 2010, making coffee was a group of friends," Clerc says of that time. He compares it to a hobby, like skateboarding. "You take your board and you go and you meet a bunch of dudes—you're doing your thing and you're having a good time all together." Like Tran in those early days, he says, "You go, 'Oh! Skateboarding is a cool thing.' And I think coffee is exactly as cool as skateboarding—as complicated, as demanding, and as cool."

The focus of Paris's old coffee culture was not quality. This explains why in Paris of all places the coffee was so bad: because the goal was something else. And yet the lingering conversation and regular community expressed in the Parisian cafe has formed the seedbed for specialty coffee to grow up in small shops between the bistros.

Friendships, like the ones fostered at Frog Fight, have helped specialty coffee in Paris grow over the past decade. It worked. And this has come at a cost. "Coffee became big and maybe there is a bit less of easy interaction. They're afraid that they now have secrets that they don't want to share," Clerc says. "I miss this a bit in coffee nowadays: all the coffee lovers meeting at some point to just have beers and chit chat about things. As soon as all those kids had their own coffee shops and their own problems and their own things, all these nice moments disappeared."

If specialty coffee is going to last in Paris it will have to become Parisian. In the long run, foreign enclaves cannot cut it. As specialty coffee gets big in Paris it may just be that the drink is at its best when it is not the goal, and the path forward lies in the past.

—

Chung-Leng Tran, Hexagone Café

Noir Coffee Shop & Torréfacteur

Un Petit Cafe With a Side of Paris

WORDS
Dale Arden Chong

PHOTOGRAPHS
Antúria Castilho Viotto

Paris knows exactly what it holds for the world to experience. With a rich cultural history, opulence, and everything else that adds to the city's *je ne sais quoi*, one thing is clear: Big things happen in the City of Light, where it seems as though the sky's the limit.

However, bring your gaze down to the street level and you'll see that, like most cities around the world, this is where everything begins. With the busyness of the city shuffling through Paris's 20 *arrondissements*, its streets teem with people and moments to watch—and it's perhaps for this very reason that purveyors pause their days to enjoy a cup of coffee amidst it all.

It's a familiar scene here: A man or woman sits at a table just off a Parisian street, with chairs facing away from the cafe and towards the happenings around it. There may be a newspaper and a pastry involved, but almost always, there's a cup of coffee. Paris is known for many things, but coffee—which is simply part of the lifestyle, according to some—is not one of them. Not yet, at least.

"France is obviously known for its gastronomy and gourmet culture, and Paris maybe drives the best representation of the French lifestyle with many cliches—among them, *le petit noir* drink while sitting on the sidewalk," Stephane Vilaysack, the co-founder of Nuance Café on the Rive Gauche in the 5th *arrondissement*, said. "But if you are a coffee lover and if you've ever been to Paris, you'll be surprised by the poor quality of this beverage. As coffee enthusiasts, we wanted to be part of the third wave of specialty coffee in Paris."

Noir Coffee Shop & Torréfacteur co-owner Martin Gunther notices that people are drinking more and more whole-bean coffee at home, indicating that the third wave of high-quality, specialty coffee is making its way through the city. "Coffee shops are a relatively new thing in Paris, in a sense that historically, people drink coffee in a traditional Parisian *brasserie*," he said. "With this perspective, coffee shops are targeting different types of people, [ones] seeking good roasts, while traditional cafes are more 'atmosphere places.' Coffee [in cafes] is bad in terms of quality [of] the bean and lack of staff training." But with businesses like Gunther's and other specialty roasters, Paris's coffee scene is quickly changing—and improving. And as it does, one thing has remained constant: the sidewalk cafe.

Outdoor dining is definitely an important part of the Parisian experience, according to Gunther, who launched three locations of his business in West Paris with his partner Guillaume Paillot de Montabert during the Covid-19 pandemic. Leaning into the city's love for the outdoors, the two opened their shops with take-away counters so their customers could enjoy their coffee outside. "It's for the *joie de vivre*. Parisians love to get together with their friends on outdoor terraces and chat. It's a rather old tradition—we use our outdoor dining spaces in the winter as we do in the summer." Of course, there's a practical reason for this. Gregoire Reversé, who co-founded Dose—which has locations in Mouffetard in the 5th *arrondissement*, and Batignolles in the 17th—with his cousin, Jean-Baptiste Déprez, attributed the city's outdoor seating trend to a lack of space. "Establishments are generally very small in Paris, and terraces allow them to have more tables," he explained.

While many cafes and coffee shops around the world have been adjusting to outdoor dining by building new structures and coverings on the sidewalks and streets to comply with

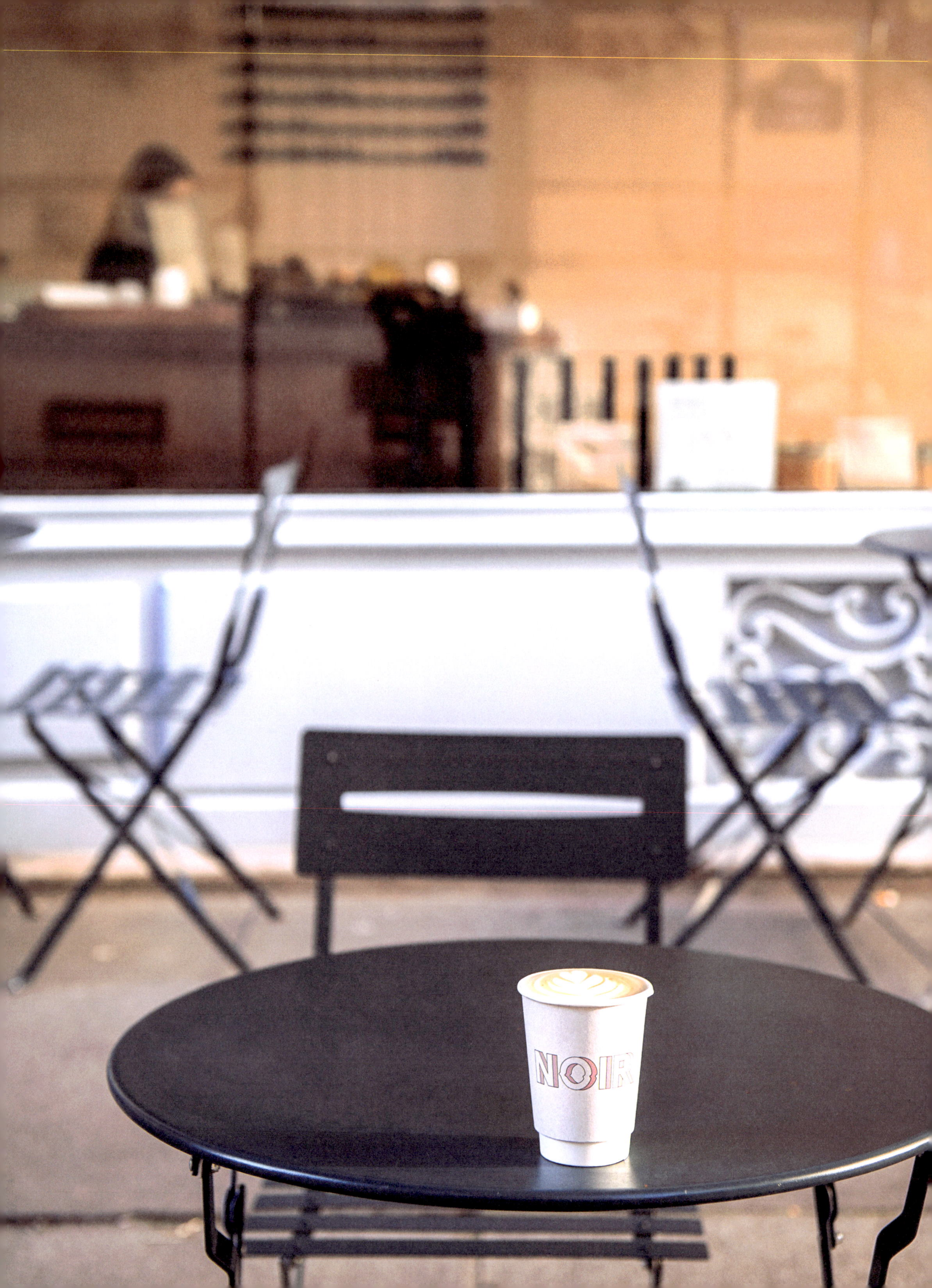
NOIR

CHAUSSURES
SUR
MESURE
HOMMES
DAMES
ENFANTS
—
FANTAISIES
POUR LA
VILLE & CÉRÉMONIE

pandemic protocols, Paris was already a step ahead, thanks to its cafe culture. In fact, the pandemics only emphasized how much Parisians enjoy being outside. "There are many jokes about it, but Parisians, even when the weather is only a little good, love to be outdoors, especially for food and coffee," Vilaysack said.

With that in mind, it came as no surprise that the city was quick to allow businesses to expand their outdoor seating beyond the sidewalk. After the first wave of the pandemic, according to Reversé, Paris's Mayor Anne Hidalgo allowed cafes to extend their terraces to the nearest outside parking spaces. This allowance was initially meant to be temporary, but the city council recently decided it will now be a recurring allowance for businesses from spring through autumn—indicating that outdoor dining is expected to become more popular in the city.

Small neighborhood spots might be the first place one thinks of when imagining the humble sidewalk setup: rows of chairs and tables organized side-by-side. However, even larger establishments have adopted this layout, Reversé noted. "What is very funny is that bigger cafes with a lot of outdoor dining space continue to place their customers facing the [street]. It is a way for customers to see the population and, above all, be seen," he said. And now, cafes of all sizes, including Noir Coffee Shop & Torréfacteur and Nuance, are designed with this idea in mind. "Our architect, who specializes in restaurant design, said people like to watch what is happening on the street, but they also like to be watched," Vilaysack shared. "This is obviously part of the French *art de vivre*."

L'art de vivre—the art of living—is a phrase used to describe the Parisian lifestyle. And yet, because it encompasses so much, the concept is hard to define it concretely. But, whether you're a resident or visitor, you'll know it when you see it: It's in the coffee and the atmosphere of every cafe. It's right there on the sidewalk, where people are watching the world—and they'll be ready for you to see them too.

—

Coffee Shop & Torre

Dose

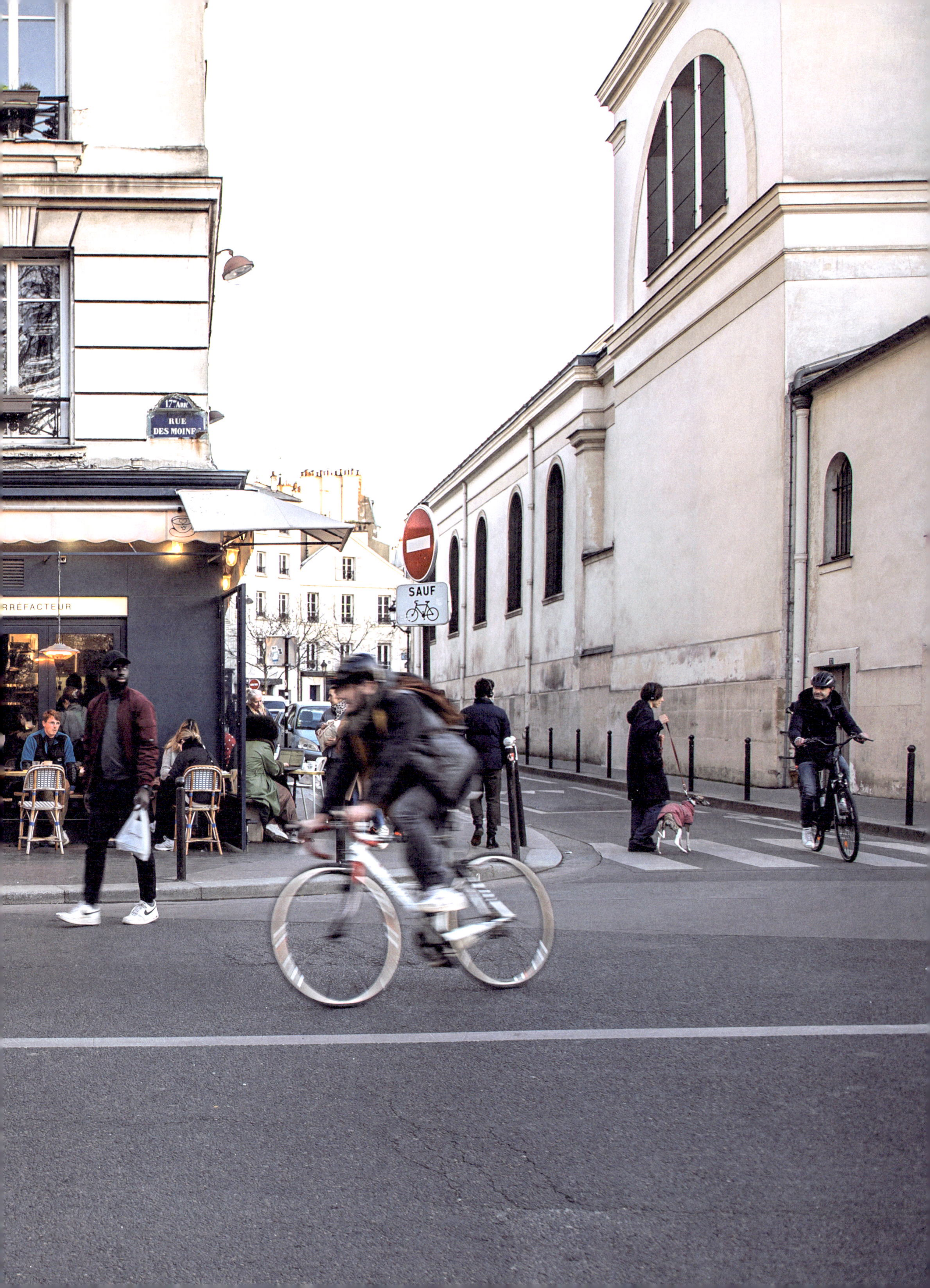
17ME ARR.
RUE
DES MOINES
RRÉFACTEUR
SAUF

Café de Flore

À La Mode

WORDS
Lane Nieset

PHOTOGRAPHS
Augusta Sagnelli

On my first trip to Paris as a study abroad student, Café de Flore was on the top of my list of must-visit places. The 19th century landmark in the well-heeled neighborhood of Saint-Germain-des-Prés is how many of us envision Paris: the corner cafe with its red leather banquettes and Art Deco-style brass fixtures and mirrored walls, feeling both intimate and like a spectacle. You're not coming for the coffee. You're coming for the history, to mimic the motions of the 20th century writers, painters and philosophers like Picasso and Hemingway, who immortalized the city's iconic cafe culture. And, of course, you're coming for the fashion. Everyone from Karl Lagerfeld to Yves Saint Laurent and his many muses held court here, and brands like Chanel, Chloé, and Paco Rabanne transformed the cafe into a runway show.

Café de Flore is still every bit as fashionable—and was somewhere I frequented on Sunday mornings when I briefly lived in the *quartier*—but with the emergence of lifestyle-themed concept shops like Merci and The Broken Arm, with their adjacent coffee shops, and Maison Kitsuné's new roastery in the Marais, fashion brands are proving that the coffee itself is just as important as the atmosphere surrounding it. "You have these places that are focusing on third wave coffee, but they also want to break down the institutionalized fourth wall of what it means to be a shop or boutique," says Paris-based Sudeep Rangi, whose work in bioethics covers the social and cultural history of food, and who is a brand creative and strategist for the legendary Parisian bakery Poilâne. "You're seeing this influence of streetwear in high fashion; they're deconstructing these identities, so it only makes sense that they're also deconstructing the physical spaces as well."

This was the design philosophy for Parisian beauty brand L'Officine Universelle Buly in its Marais boutique, which opened in 2017. It shares a space with the revived Grand Café Tortoni. Once a 19th century meeting place for artists, writers, and socialites, the cafe was revived here on the rue de Saintonge with an interior designed to recall the Belle Èpoque era (the original cafe was in Paris's Golden Triangle in the 8th *arrondissement*). On the left is an apothecary-inspired jade-green marble cosmetics counter. Lining the wall behind it are floor-to-ceiling, glass-paneled oak cabinets beautifully displaying Berber natural lipstick, customizable tortoiseshell-patterned combs, and L'Officine Universelle Buly's signature white bottles of perfume and oils. On the right side, antique-style wooden stools line the cafe's bar. A menu of homemade ice cream and *café minute* (coffee made-to-order) etched into marble slabs is displayed on the wall behind the bar and is served by women in pleated skirts resembling something a headmistress may have worn in eras past.

Founders Ramdane Touhami and Victoire de Taillac scoured eBay and antique markets across France to source the cafe's vintage silver trays and Limoges porcelain cups, while coffee hails from their neighborhood roaster Brûlerie de Varenne in the 7th *arrondissement*. "The coffee culture has changed so much in the past 10 years, and everyone is starting to pay more attention to the quality of what we're drinking," says de Taillac. "Traditional [neighborhood] cafes are still so much a part of French culture, since they're next to your home and where you'll go to meet friends for coffee in the morning or a drink at night. This is still quite strong, but different from what newer spots are offering. Now, when you go into a shop [that has a cafe], it's like another service you can get."

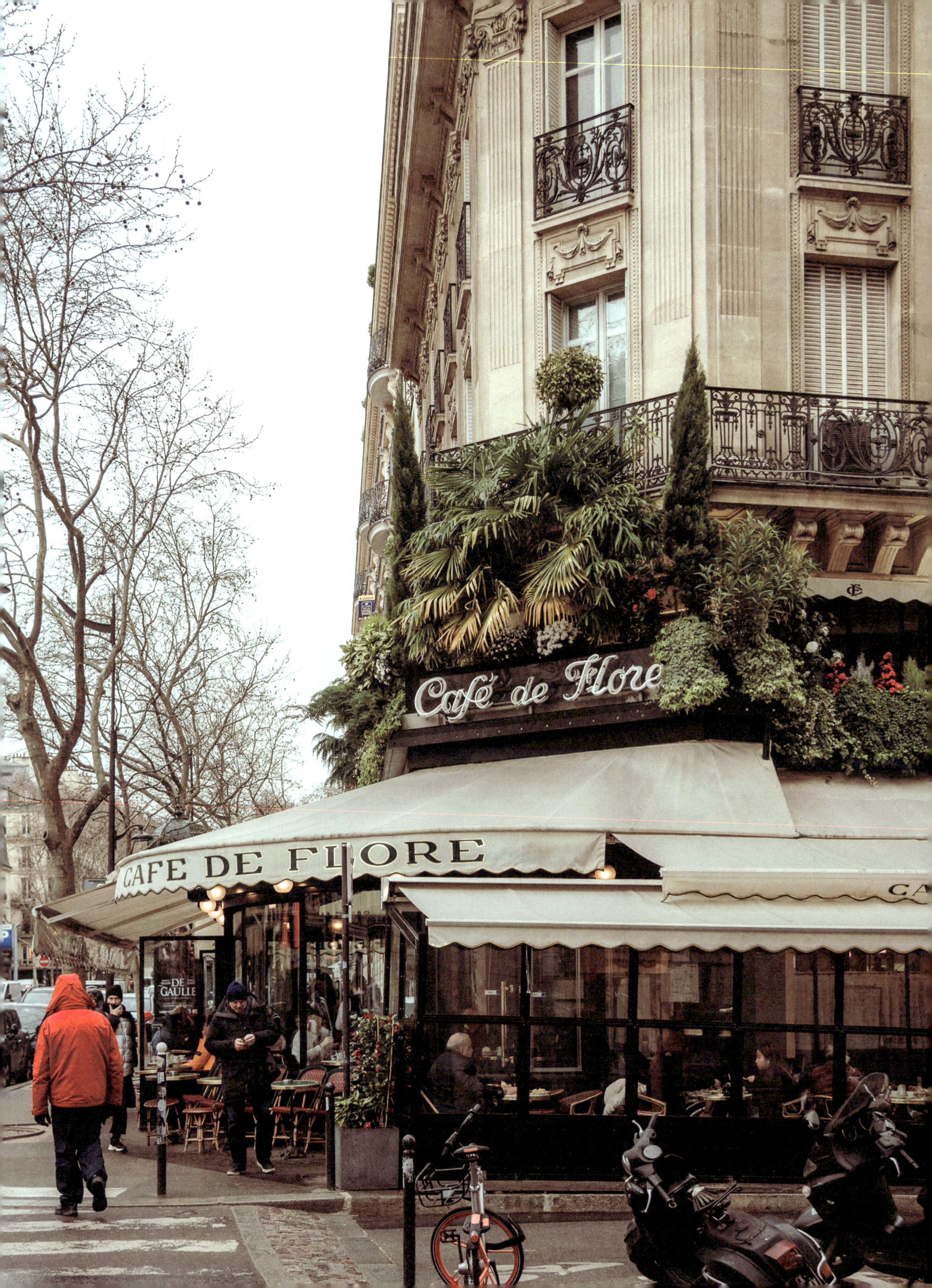
Café de Flore
CAFE DE FLORE
DE GAULLE

Café de Flore
PARIS
menu
Café de Flore
Café de Flore
Saint Germain des Prés
Tél. 01.45.48.55.26
JMB PARIS

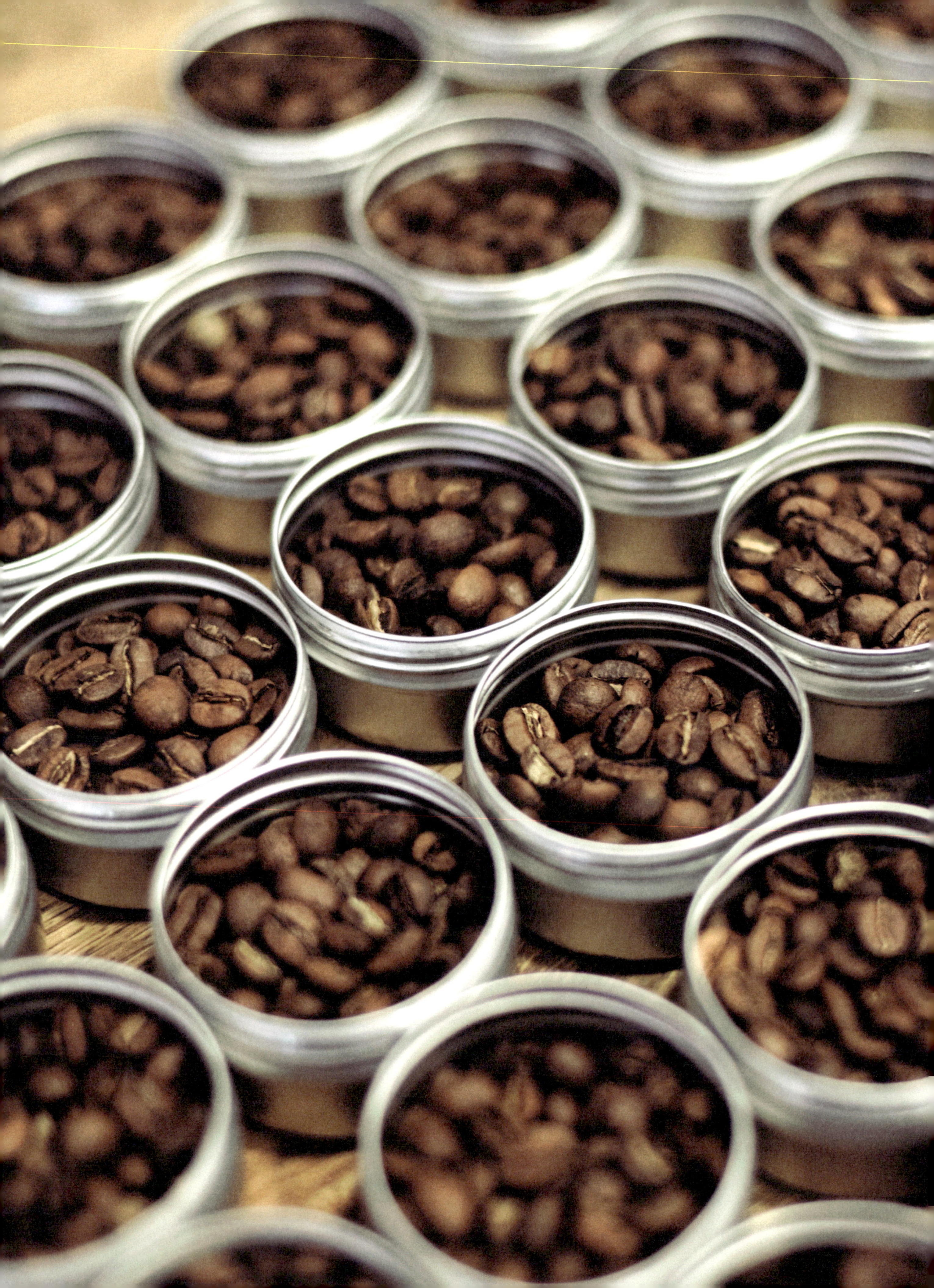

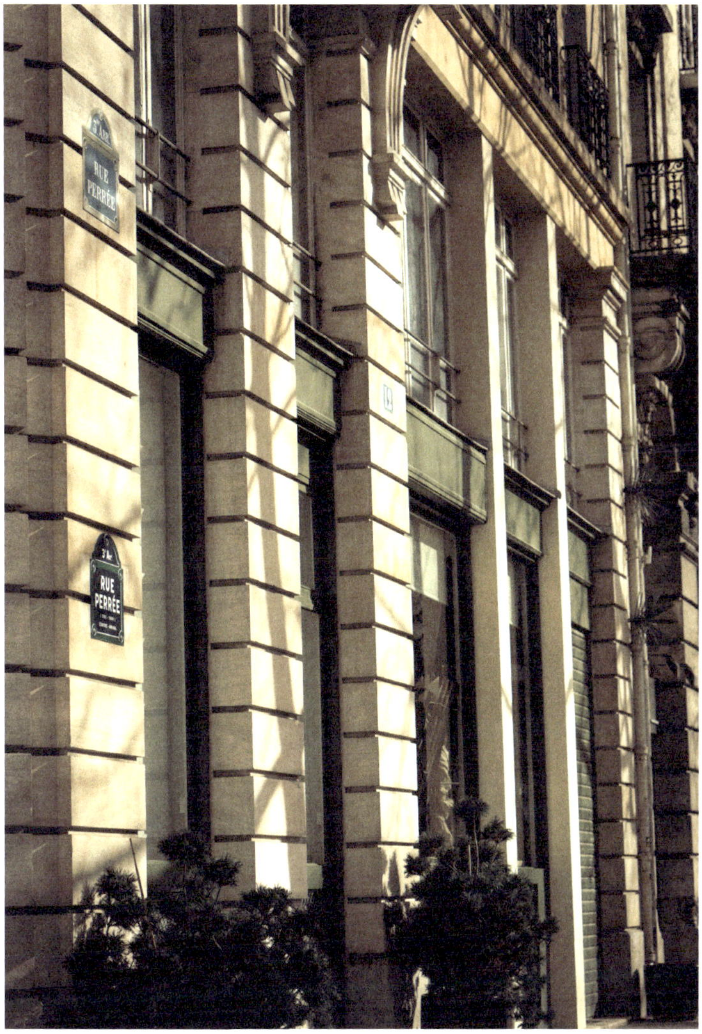

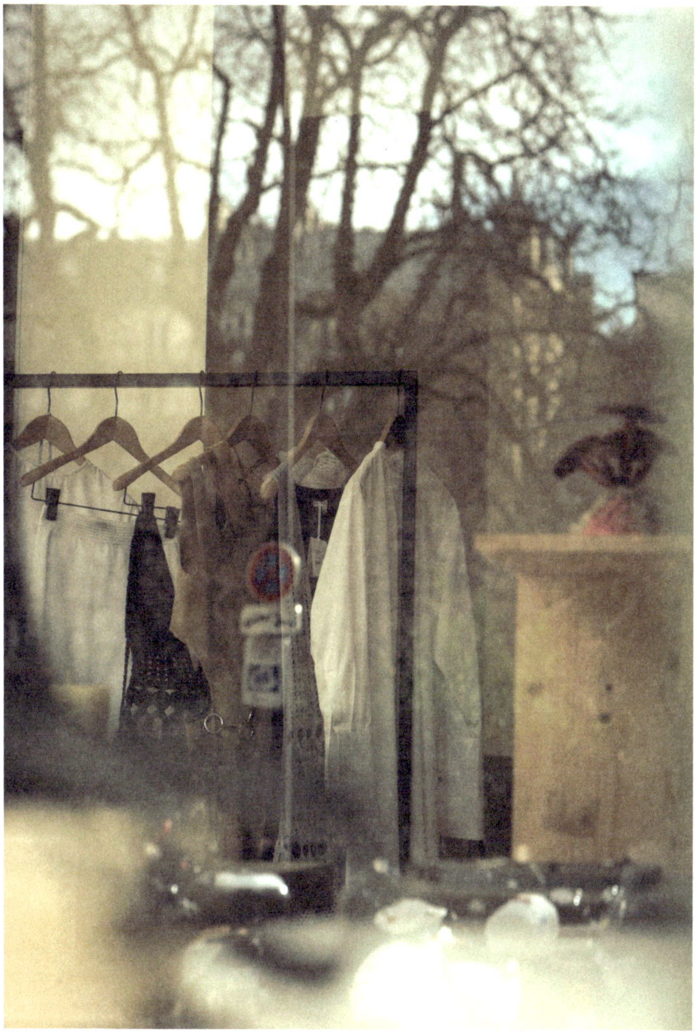

Grand Café Tortoni

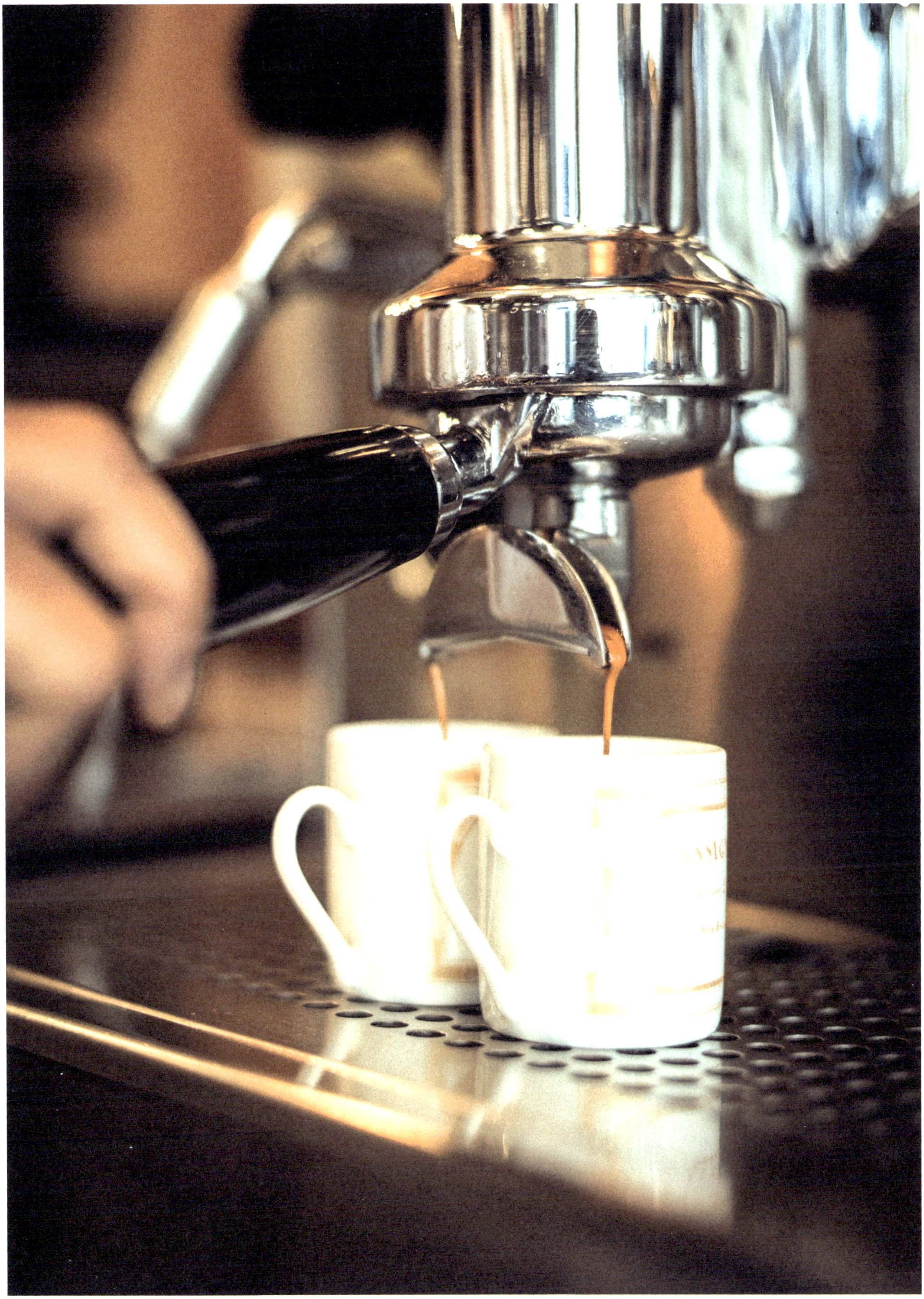

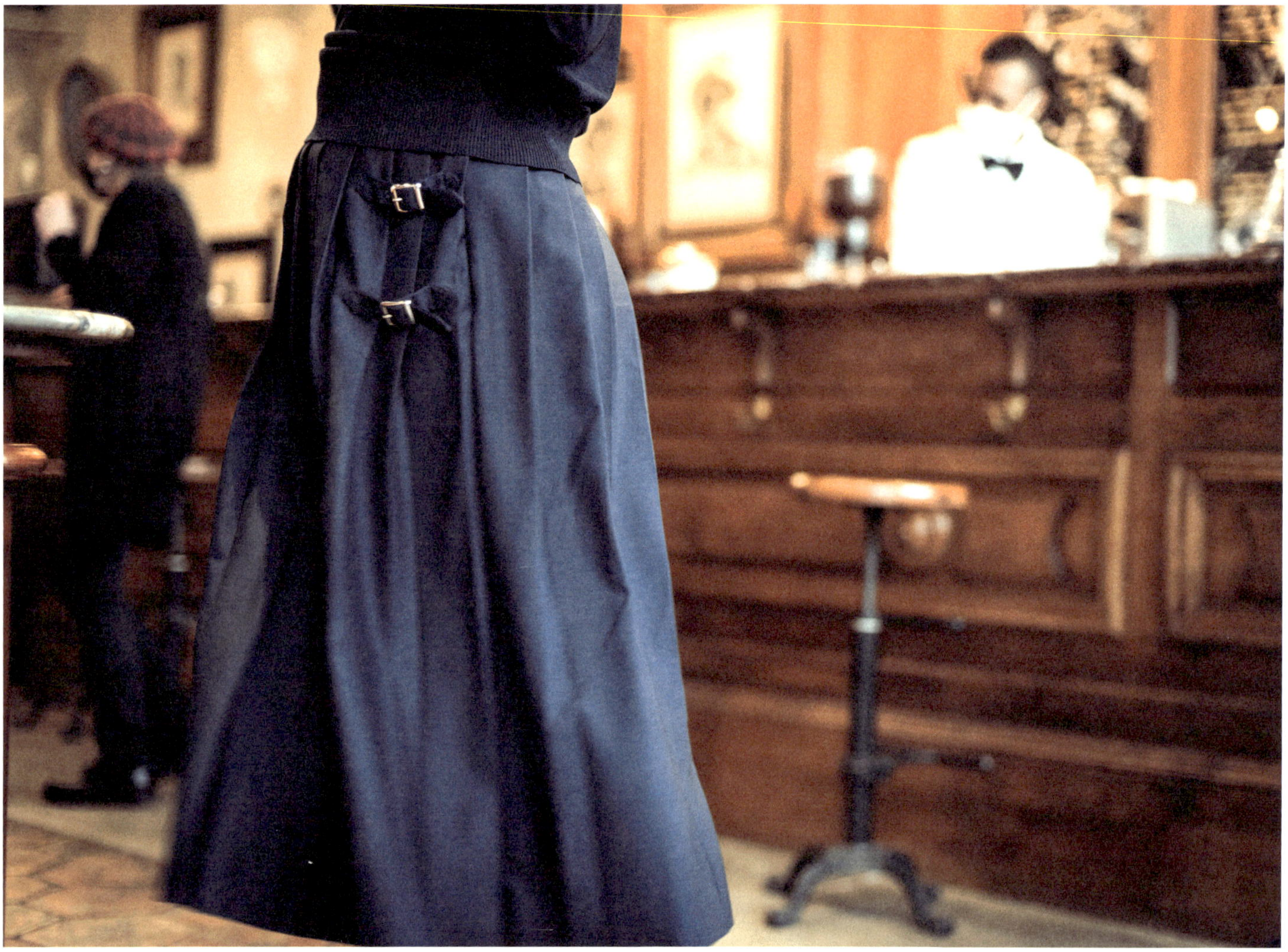

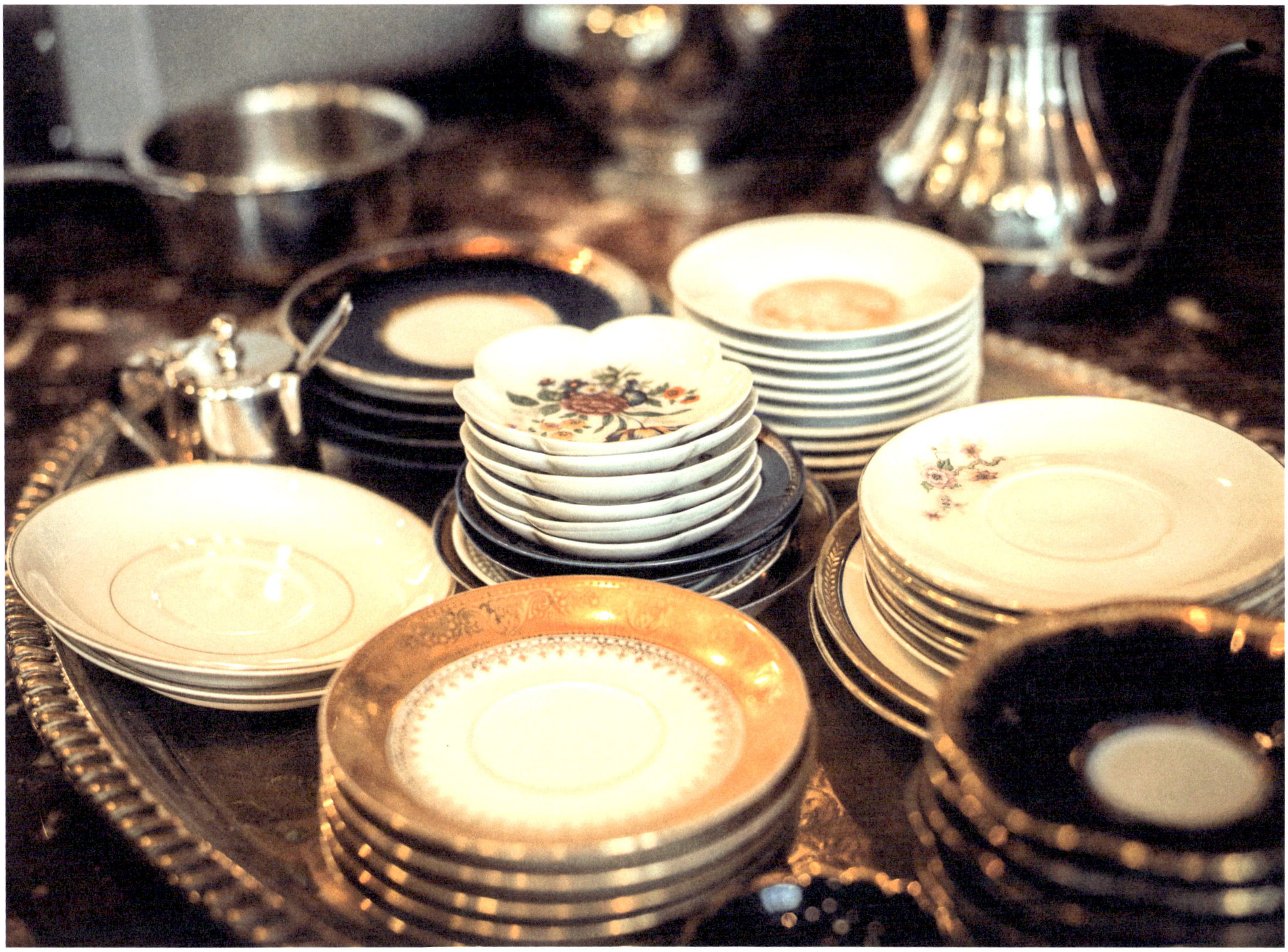

84 — PARIS   Officine Universelle Buly

PARIS — 85

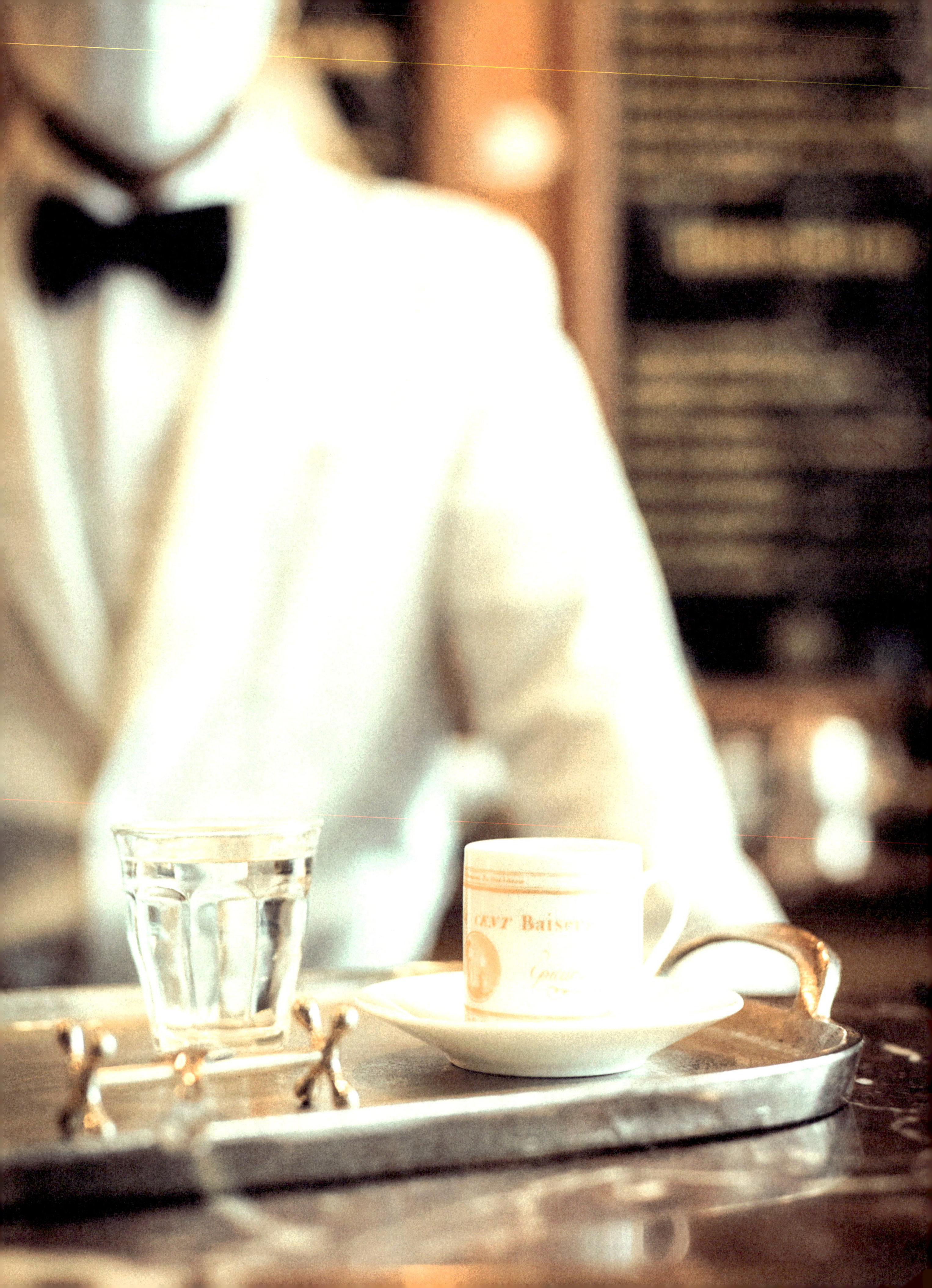
Baiser

On a recent chilly winter morning, I went to visit Belleville Brûlerie, one of the city's leading roasteries. The cafe and roaster is run by the team behind my old neighborhood coffee shop, Le 50 in Belleville, which sadly shuttered during Paris's first pandemic lockdown. Head coffee roaster, Bucharest-born Mihaela Iordache, has spent the past eight years working her way up in the Paris specialty coffee scene—and earned the coveted title of Roast Masters Champion in 2019 in the process. She talked about how Belleville Brûlerie was one of the first in the country to rethink coffee blends within a specialty coffee environment to "distance ourselves from what used to be the old coffee houses with no traceability or transparency. We saw this as a great opportunity to tell stories with coffee [through blends], and there's something very special and French about *l'art de l'assemblage*," she says.

In French culture, there's *assemblage*, or blending, in everything from flour for bread to wines for Champagne and Cognac. "It's interesting that a coffee that's not French in origin can be Parisian because of its blend, its DNA," she says, adding that what also feels French is the traditional corner cafes with their Old World atmosphere. "This is a culture that's nostalgic about the beauty of its past. When I go somewhere like L'Officine Universelle Buly, I'm in awe of the space itself; it immediately feels Parisian to me."

There has been an explosion of roasters over the past few years in Paris. And now, places that were importing concepts and architecture from coffee capitals like London or Copenhagen want to create a Parisian identity, bringing specialty coffee to traditional Parisian spaces. "It's no longer just this New Age, industrial open vibe that is a signifier of 'good coffee' in the city," Rangi says. "There's the pressure or interest in locavorism, and the idea that if roasting is being done here, it feels more local."

When Maison Kitsuné launched 20 years ago, it started as a music label (founded by the Franco-Japanese duo Gildas Loaëc, who was one of Daft Punk's managers, and Masaya Kuroki) before morphing into a fashion brand and coffee shop that's one of the best definitions of *l'art de vivre*. When the original cafe in Paris opened in the Palais Royal gardens in 2011, Maison Kitsuné was one of the first fashion brands in the city to debut a specialty coffee shop. To create a link between Café Kitsuné and the Parisian fashion house, Maison Kitsuné even created ready-to-wear clothing and accessories with the fox emblem (*kitsuné* means fox in Japanese) and a color palette of matcha-green and latte-beige to match the brand's signature drinks.

In 2021, Maison Kitsuné also opened its first European roastery, Café Kitsuné Vertbois, in a sleek, Scandinavian-style space in the Marais where it roasts the brand's signature house blend: a full-bodied coffee, with notes of chocolate and honey, using beans sourced in Brazil and Guatemala. And, to marry the fashion and coffee concepts, the cafe sells a line of branded tableware, including cups and saucers. "We're seeing this trend in a lot of coffee shops [in the city] roasting for themselves," Iordache explains. "I think what's happening in fashion [demonstrates] how coffee has been democratized in Paris over the past few years."

Not everyone may be roasting in-house or sporting a menu of slow coffee methods like V60 or Chemex, but boutiques that once offered nondescript espresso while you browsed four-figure bags and sky-high footwear are switching gears and placing more emphasis on the coffee they're pouring. Even Saint Laurent, which opened its first cafe next to the Rive Droite boutique near the Tuileries gardens, is serving espresso from a statement-making Faema E61, which is poured into black, branded to-go cups that are the coffee equivalent of a designer shopping bag. And as a girl who feels that "shopper's high" after making a big purchase, there's something gratifying about strolling the city with a little black cup in hand, and knowing that what I'm sipping is just as luxurious as what's sitting on the shelves in the shop.

—

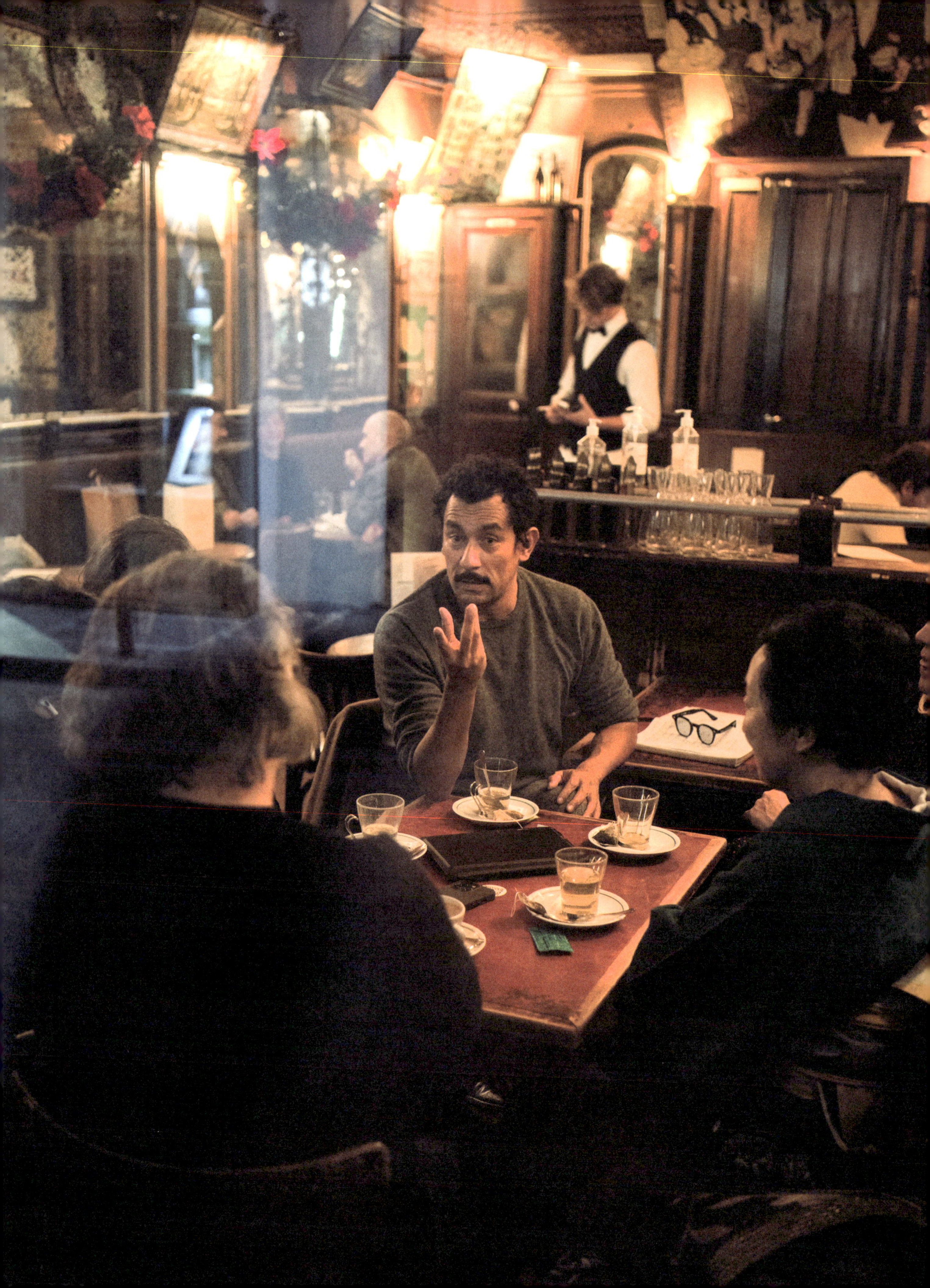

Rencontre

WORDS
Jae Lee

PHOTOGRAPHS
Julien Prebel

In Saint Germain des Pres, an indispensable tourist stopover neighborhood for its antiquated cafes, like Café de Flore or Les Deux Magots, is another monumental salon: La Palette. On rue de Seine, near the Beaux Arts Academy, the cafe is described on the Ministry of Culture's website as one "with two rooms, the first decorated with canvases and palettes offered by artist-clients, the second decorated with six ceramic panels showing the life of coffee during the 1930s or 1940s." It's a chilly Tuesday afternoon when I meet an eclectic group of artists here—interviewing them on behalf of Drift Magazine—to reflect on the French artist cafe culture of the past and present. From the president of Balthus Atelier to an art historian of a contemporary fashion designer, each of the five has influenced the French culture scene.

The first to arrive is Thomas Hardy, a former arts editor of Playboy Magazine, and now a curator organizing residency programs for young artists on the west coast of France. Setsuko Klossowska de Rola arrives shortly after from her ceramic *atelier* and takes a quick stroll around the neighborhood, which was depicted by her deceased husband Balthasar Klossowski de Rola (the Polish-French Modern artist known as Balthus) in his most famous painting "La Rue." As I am waiting for the others by the entrance, Emilie Bouvard, Director of Collections and Scientific Program at the Fondation Giacometti Paris, mysteriously appears in the backroom, the waiter tells me. Diana Ruiz-Picasso, an art historian and a granddaughter of Pablo Picasso, hops off the cab in a billowing dress befitting her cheerful character. As Picasso hops off, I see Haider Ackermann walking towards us. Ackermann, once praised by Karl Lagerfeld as the ideal successor for Chanel, is a go-to fashion designer for many Parisian artists and Hollywood stars.

I've gathered these five because they've worked in both past and the current French culture scenes. And on this chilly, Tuesday afternoon, with the sun setting, they reminisce about the coffee hubs of the Modernists, and to discuss how they have evolved since then.

***

Drift: Diana, when was the last time you saw Setsuko, your so-called "sister," for a coffee?

Ruiz-Picasso: It was not too long ago, on rue Jacob in July? We meet often at events, but Setsuko is like a butterfly, she's always on the road so I have to catch her for a coffee.

Klossowska de Rola: It is because I am a *poisson*, you know? A Pisces, always swimming. [Laughs.]

Ruiz-Picasso: I just went through the items my mother got from my grandfather and they were quite dusty. So I collected the dust and sent them to an archeologist. They will be able to find what he ate, smoked, or if he had any illness. My family never believed in thorough cleaning or complete renovation.

Ackermann: That's fascinating. You know one of my favorite phrases is "Excuse My Dust" on Dorothy Parker's tombstone.

Drift: Be assured Diana, no renovation will be done here. La Palette was a designated historic monument in the 1980s. I mean, there are several more around here that preserve the memory of Picasso and his gatherings.

Klossowska de Rola: Balthus adored Picasso. He visited Balthus and bought a painting when Balthus was a poor artist.

La Palette

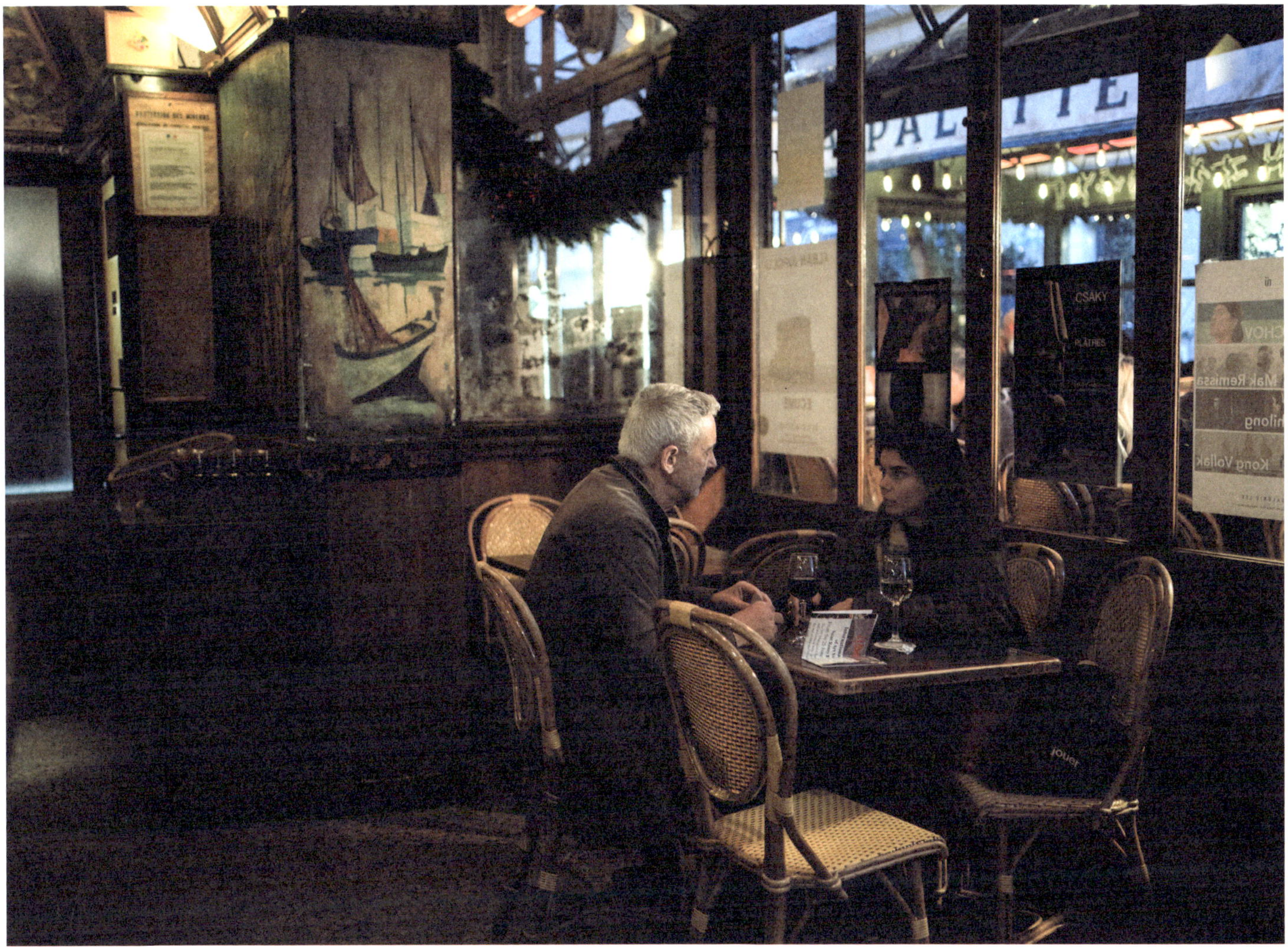
CSAKY

Diana Ruiz-Picasso

Thomas Hardy

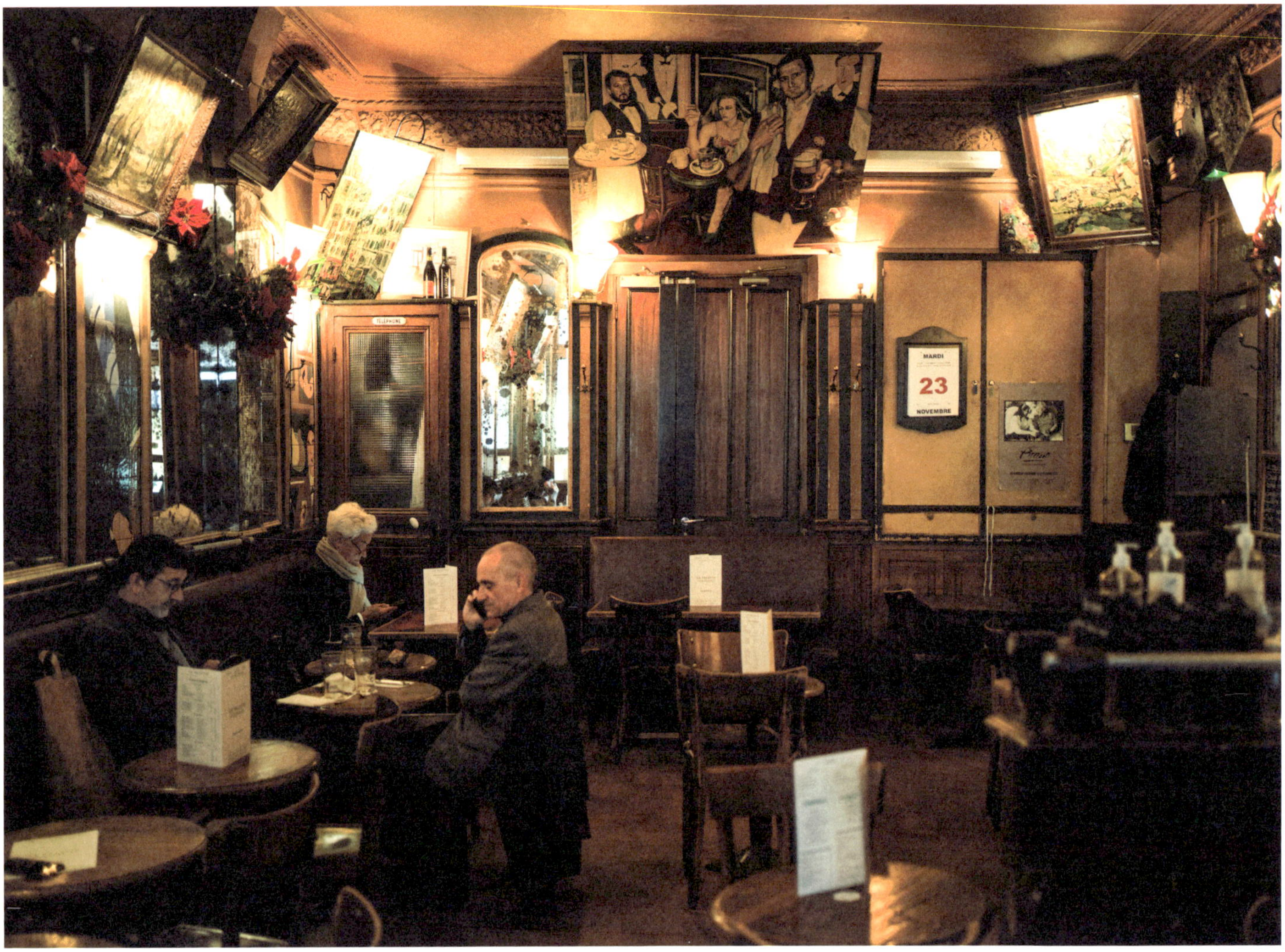
MARDI
23
NOVEMBRE

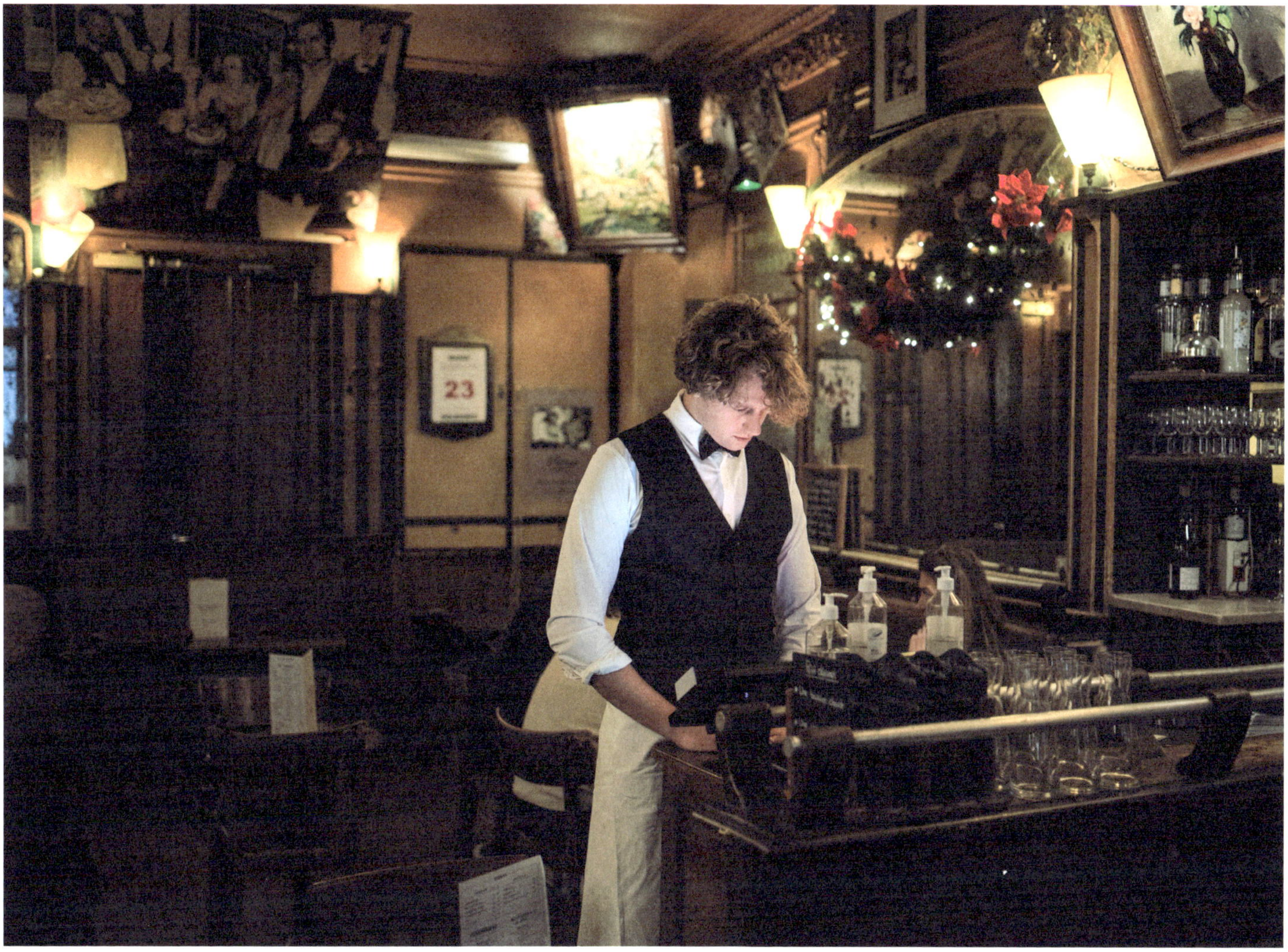

Setsuko Klossowska de Rola

Emilie Bouvard

intime
Picasso
PHOTOGRAPHIES DE JACQUELINE PICASSO
EXPOSITION DU 4 NOVEMBRE AU 12 DÉCEMBRE 2021
GALERIE DE L'INSTITUT
12 RUE DE SEINE
75006 PARIS

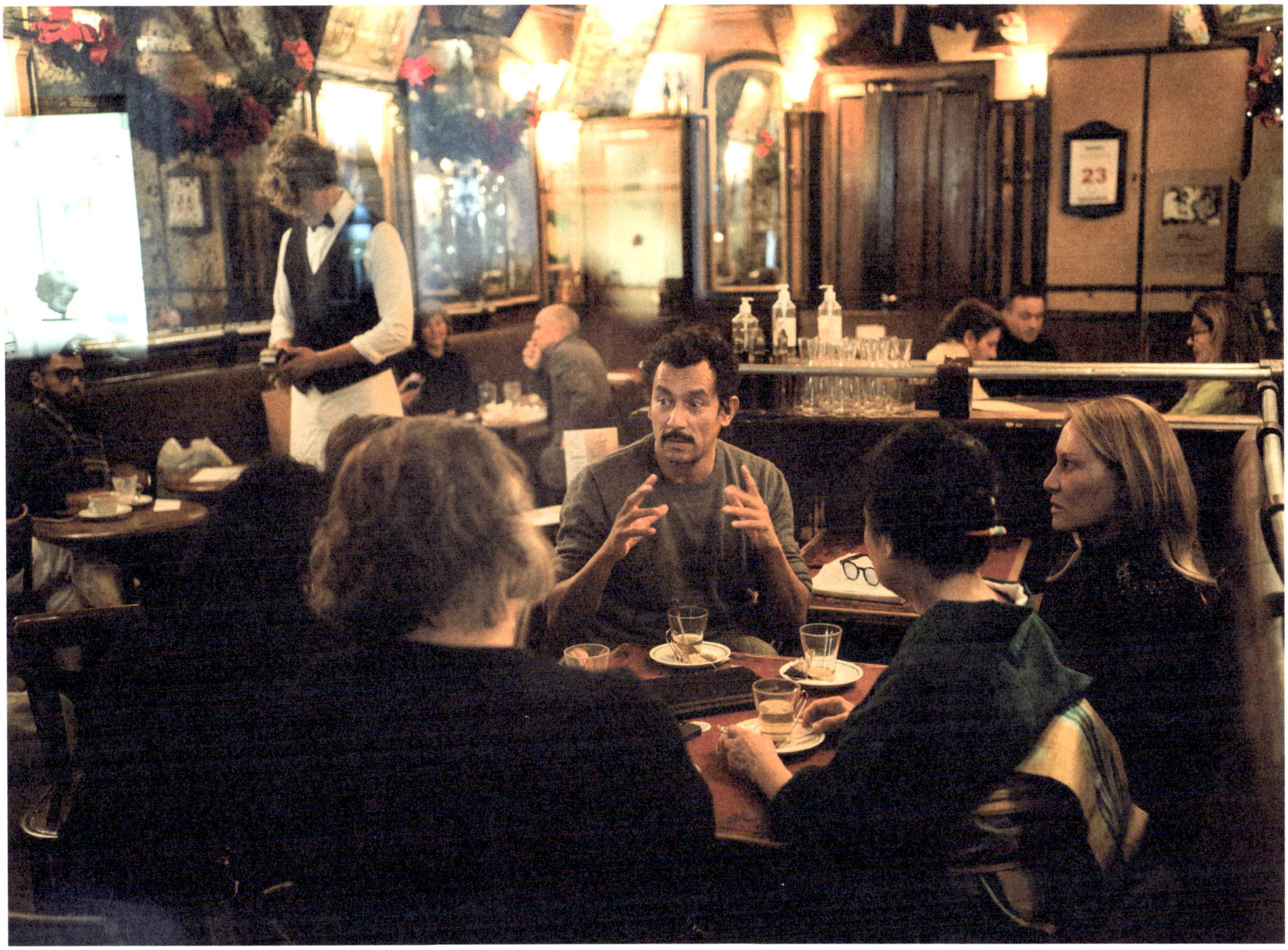

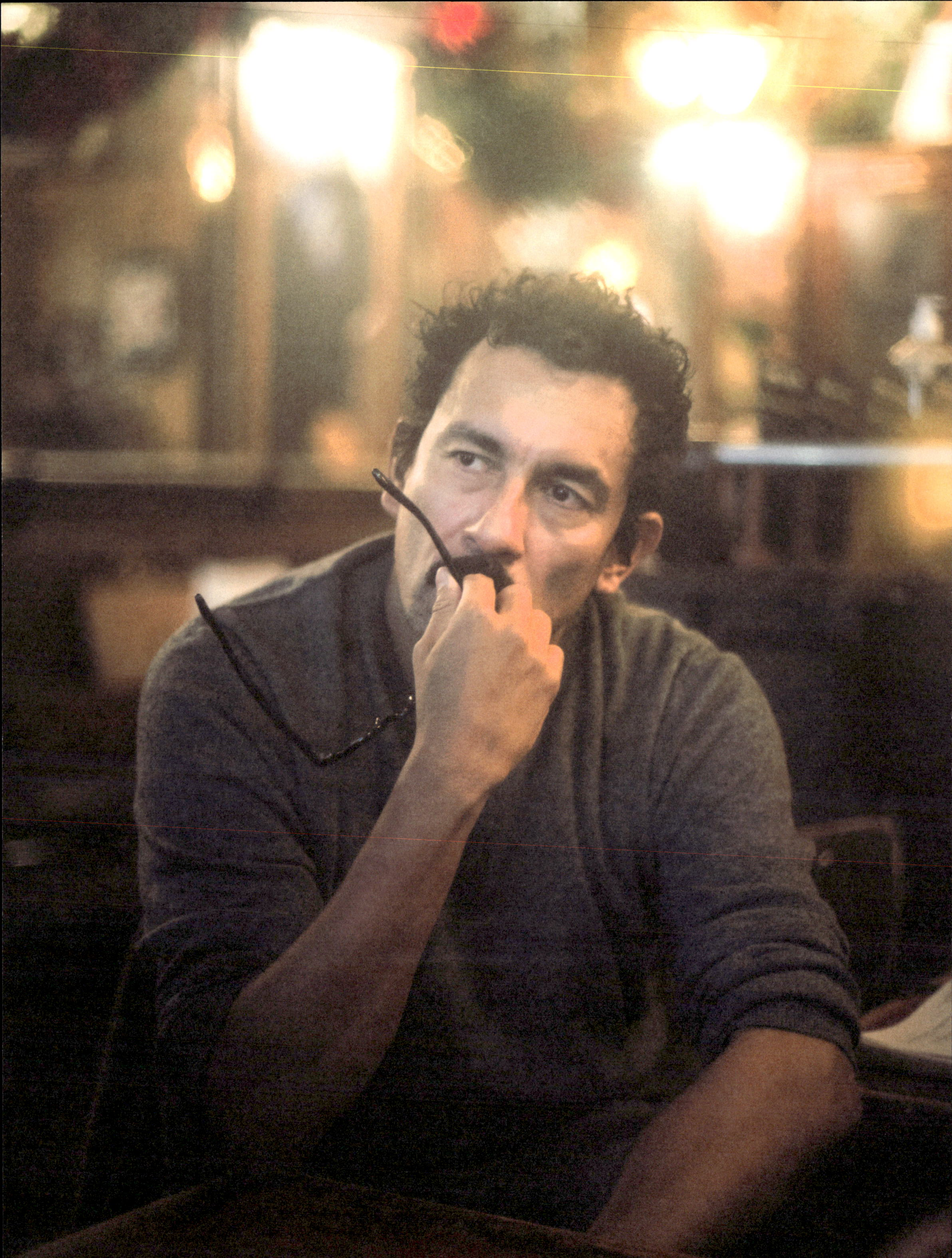

Balthus admired how a classically trained artist could draw such impactful abstractions.

Ruiz-Picasso: You know it was quite rare for my grandfather to buy works of an unknown artist, but they really developed a deep bond.

Drift: When was this?

Klossowska de Rola: Before Balthus moved to Cour du Rohan?

Bouvard: It was during the 1940s. They used to meet at cafes and draw on napkins. There was an auction dedicated to the napkin drawings by Balthus or Picasso from that year not too long ago. After Balthus left Paris, Giacometti met Picasso everyday. For him, it wasn't just a cup of coffee—it was a part of his lifestyle. He was poor, without heating in his studio or home, and he really appreciated the warmth of being inside a cafe to have a warm drink or food, and to socialize.

Ruiz-Picasso: A Spanish word *tertulia* means a gathering to discuss or debate, and my great-grandfather was deeply involved in these group gatherings in Málaga. I think my grandfather kept this tradition in Paris.

Klossowska de Rola: But the question is how we connect with other creatives today compared to the past artists of this neighborhood. Balthus used to say "art is finished" in his late career. With smartphones, it keeps us constantly busy and feeds us too much information. For example, when I had a chance to meet Thomas at the FIAC last fall, it was difficult for me to properly understand his creations as we were constantly pulled to meetings, chats, and news via smartphones.

Hardy: I am working on renovating an abandoned factory in a remote town on the west coast, where young artists will be invited to not only create, but form a community. I am like a gardener. There are big artists, and [there are] young ones, [who], like emerging plants, need a caretaker. Some need more water, while some need more sun.

Bouvard: I think this culture of gathering still exists among the younger generation of Paris. Around this area, they hop around cafes to put up exhibition posters. Of course, the internet plays a big role today as well.

Ackermann: But with social media, it's less of an exchange. The words are reduced, there is little dialogue and no dynamic. Every meeting is different and every eye is beautiful to gaze into.

Ruiz-Picasso: You must admit, it is convenient. Sometimes, it's the only way to get the job done.

Hardy: Social media [are] more cognitive. But when you meet for a coffee, there's more behavioral and emotional effort that goes in. You put your jacket on and head out.

Klossowska de Rola: I believe that life is an illusion. In this illusion, if we can find a moment to touch or hear their voice, that's quite extraordinary. The five senses of [humans are] very important when making a connection, and a must for artists.

—

What We Eat With Coffee

WORDS
J.R.M. Owens

PHOTOGRAPHS
Tom Claisse

STYLING
Karina Rikun

The enduring contribution of France to the world of coffee is not sipped but savored. Bread and pastry making, a craft older than memory, became an art form in this country. This place gave final form to croissants, and it's putting sourdough center stage in boutique bakeries. Together—pastries and bread—they are the two outstanding gifts of France to coffee.

For hundreds of years, coffee has been enjoyed with something to eat, most typically the croissant. Ubiquitous, from corner cafes to Starbucks to independent coffee shops, croissants have always been enjoyed by coffee drinkers of every persuasion and no persuasion.

The croissant originated at some point in centuries past as the *kipfel* in Vienna, and from there the pastry was brought to Paris where it became the thing we know today. It is mentioned there throughout the 19th century, beginning with the first Viennese bakery opened in 1838 by August Zang. In France the crescent-shaped bread was rendered with puff pastry and so the croissant took its present form.

With a light, lavish feel developed in Europe's capitals of luxury, the croissant became synonymous with breakfast on the continent. The hop from breakfast to coffee was then a small one. "Continental breakfast—it's coffee and croissant!" says Anthony Courteille with a laugh. Anthony is the founder and head baker at SAIN Boulangerie in the 10th *arrondissement*. "In Paris, croissant is for breakfast. And at breakfast, you drink coffee in general. Coffee and croissant—it's a pair."

That pair is "really a French tradition," says Julien Cantenot, founder of Atelier P1 in the 18th *arrondissement*. "That's the first thing people buy in the morning."

Sain Boulangerie

Sain Boulangerie

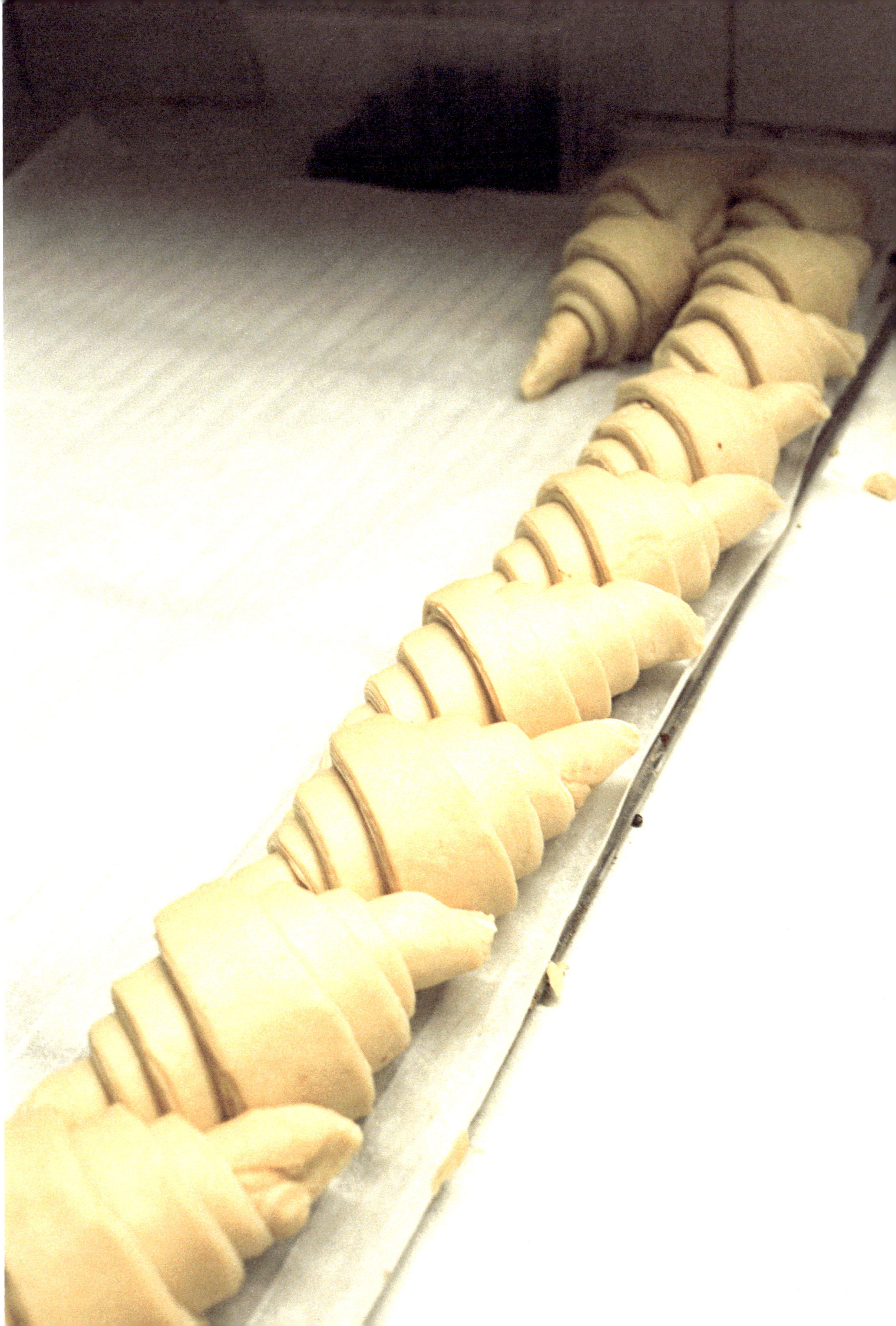

Ten Belles

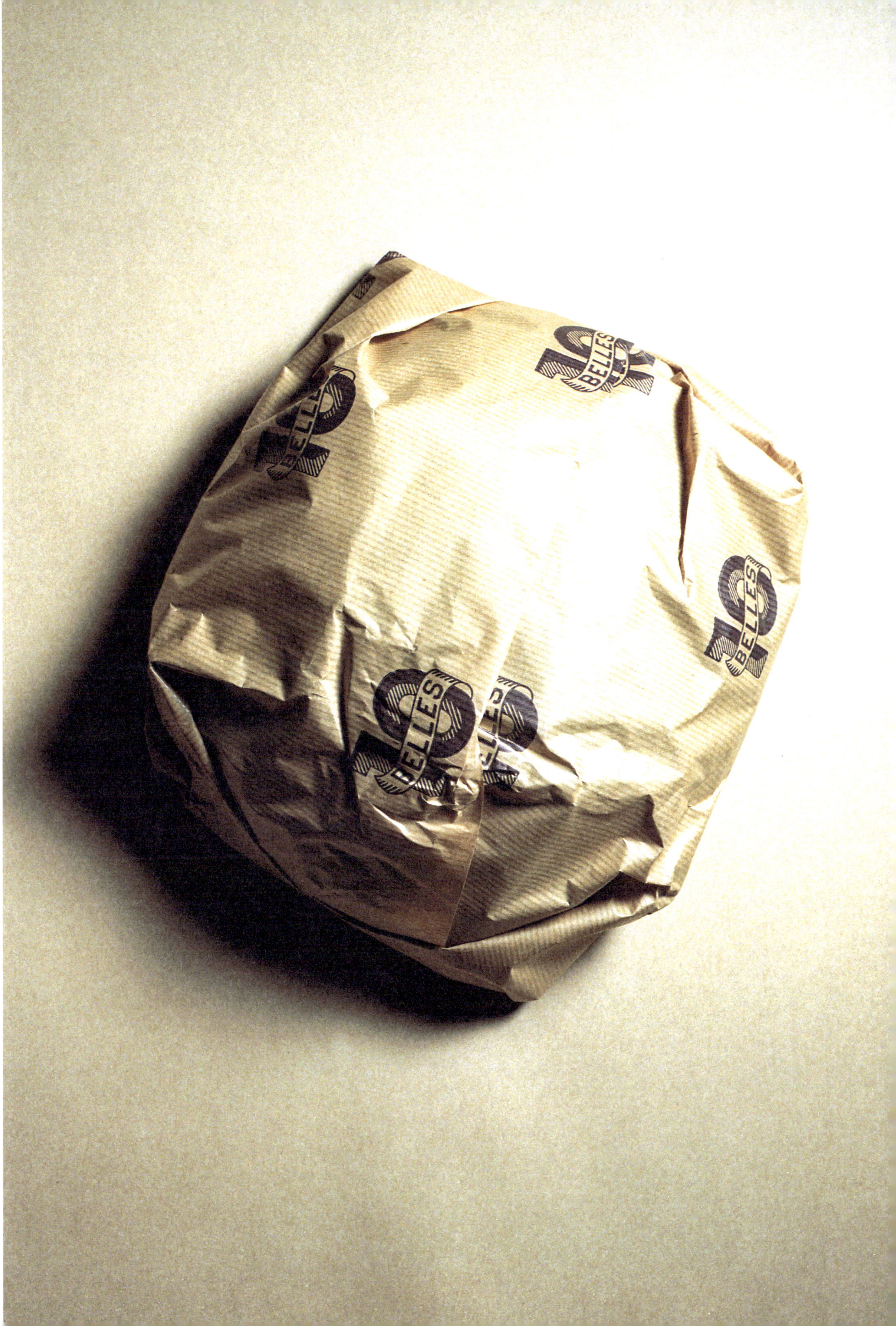
BELLES

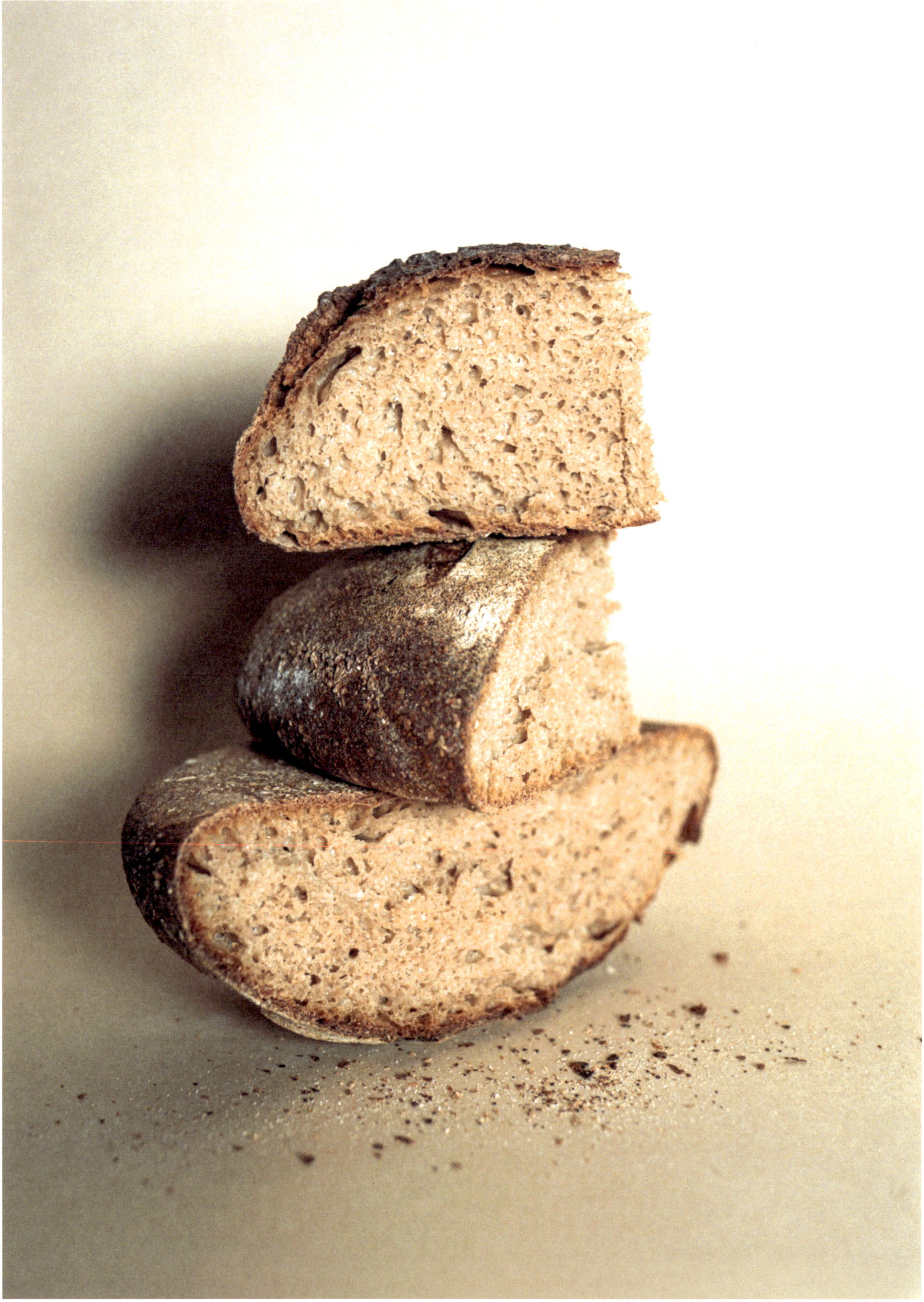

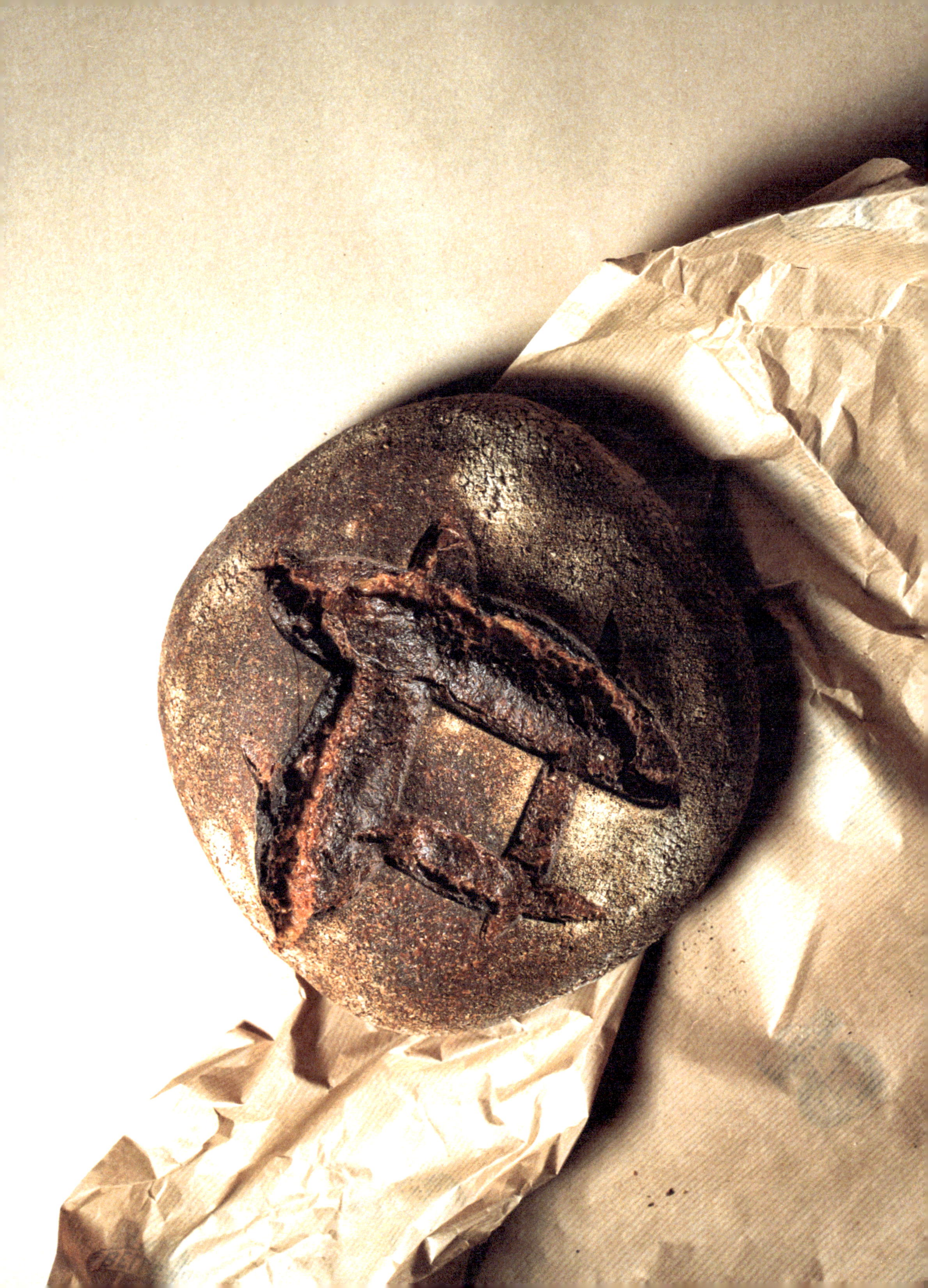

Chanceux

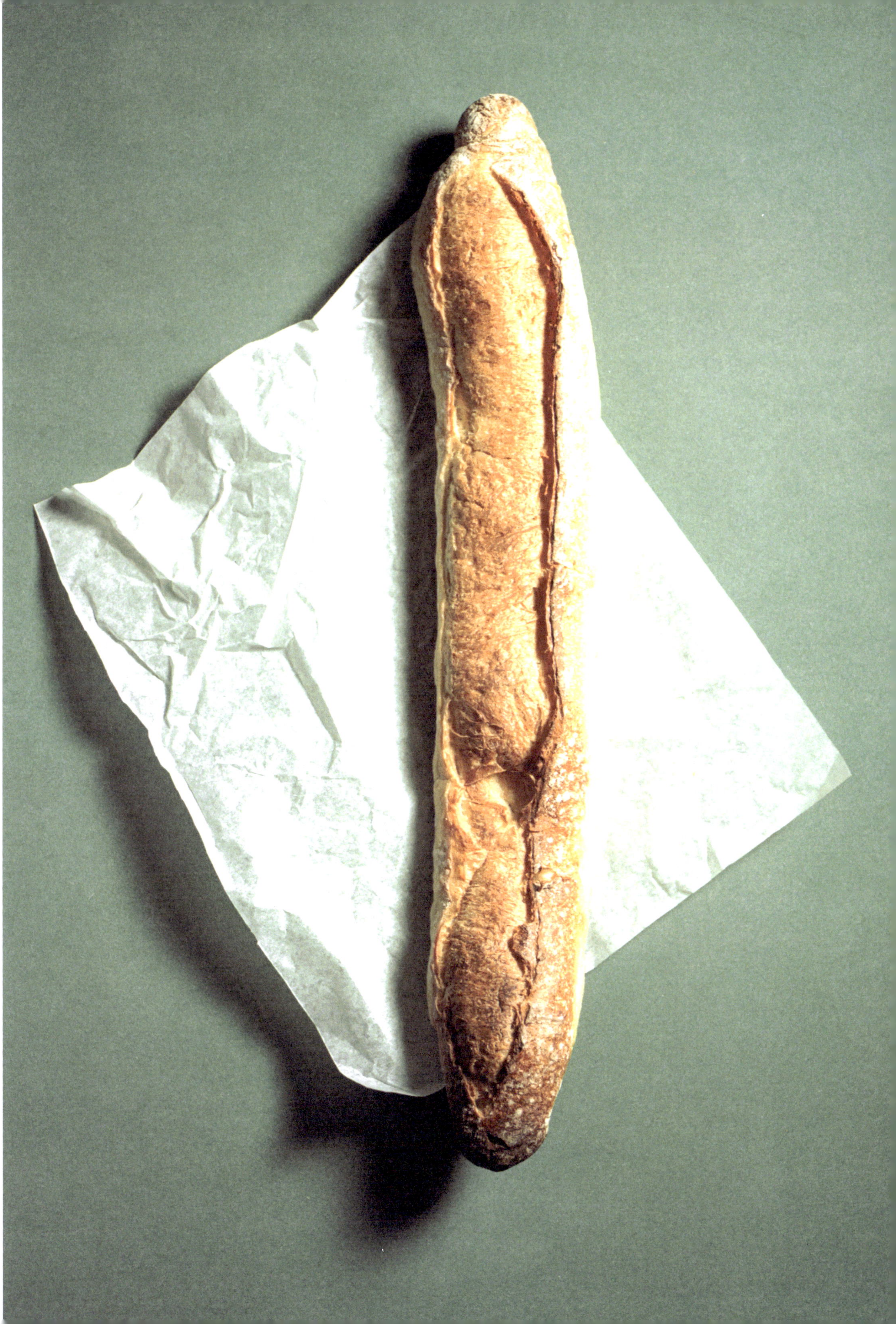

And that tradition has spread throughout the world, having been passed down for centuries, as coffee shops everywhere now serve croissants from glass countertop cases.

With the third wave of coffee came the revival of another French gift. In recent years, sourdough bread has been appearing beside coffee. The two are mostly found together in coffee shops that serve food, like sandwiches and sometimes wine as well. Ten Belles (with locations in the 6th, 10th, and 11th *arrondissements*) would be illustrative.

Before the rise of brewers and commercial yeasts, all bread was made from sourdough, which uses wild yeasts found in the air to naturally ferment and leaven bread dough. Then around the time of World War II, commercial yeasts took over around the globe. These fast-acting yeasts cut the fermentation time of bread, allowing bakers to work in the early morning hours, rather than throughout the night. Bakers could begin work around 3:00 AM, rather than 11:00 PM. "It was better," says Julien. "Everyone wants to have a normal life with a family, especially because there's a lot of work in this business."

The move from natural to commercial fermentation meant "you can [make a] croissant or… bread, or baguette in two hours. You can do it very fast," says Courteille. "Step by step," he says, the big companies offered to make bakers' work easier, and as the time decreased so too the quality fell.

"There is no natural fermentation and it's very hard to digest," Courteille says. "It's like wine." Over the decades and beginning with the yeast, the line between local baker and commercial production blurred. "There is no difference between [an] industrial bakery and a bakery on the street. They use the same products."

In recent decades sourdough has sprung up in artisanal bakeries and home kitchens around the globe. San Francisco is perhaps the epicenter of this revival, with sourdough in lore and substance dating to the mid-19th century. And here again France comes in, for it was French bakers, such as Isidore Boudin, who applied their knowledge of the craft to the bread and pancakes that fed the California Gold Rush in the 1800s.

The revival of natural fermentation in breadmaking has coincided with the third wave in coffee. There is inherently synergy in the two, as they both focus on natural sourcing and methodology. While prior waves of coffee focused on the bean as commodity or on the customer as consumer, third wave coffee culture tends to speak of the drink with a vinous attention to quality. As Cantenot puts it, "Specialty coffee is really the same approach to the coffee that sourdough is to bread—the will to do things really properly." So it's not surprising to find the two served together. The kind of person curious about natural processing in coffee happens often to be the same person concerned about natural fermentation in bread.

In the perennial appeal of croissants and the revival of sourdough, France has made substantive contributions to some of the most common foods that go with coffee. Everywhere coffee is enjoyed, from sidewalk bistros to Starbucks to the third wave archetype, bread and pastries are sure to be to be found. Perfected over the centuries, it's the craft of France's bakeries that has so well complemented the world of coffee.

—

Chanceux

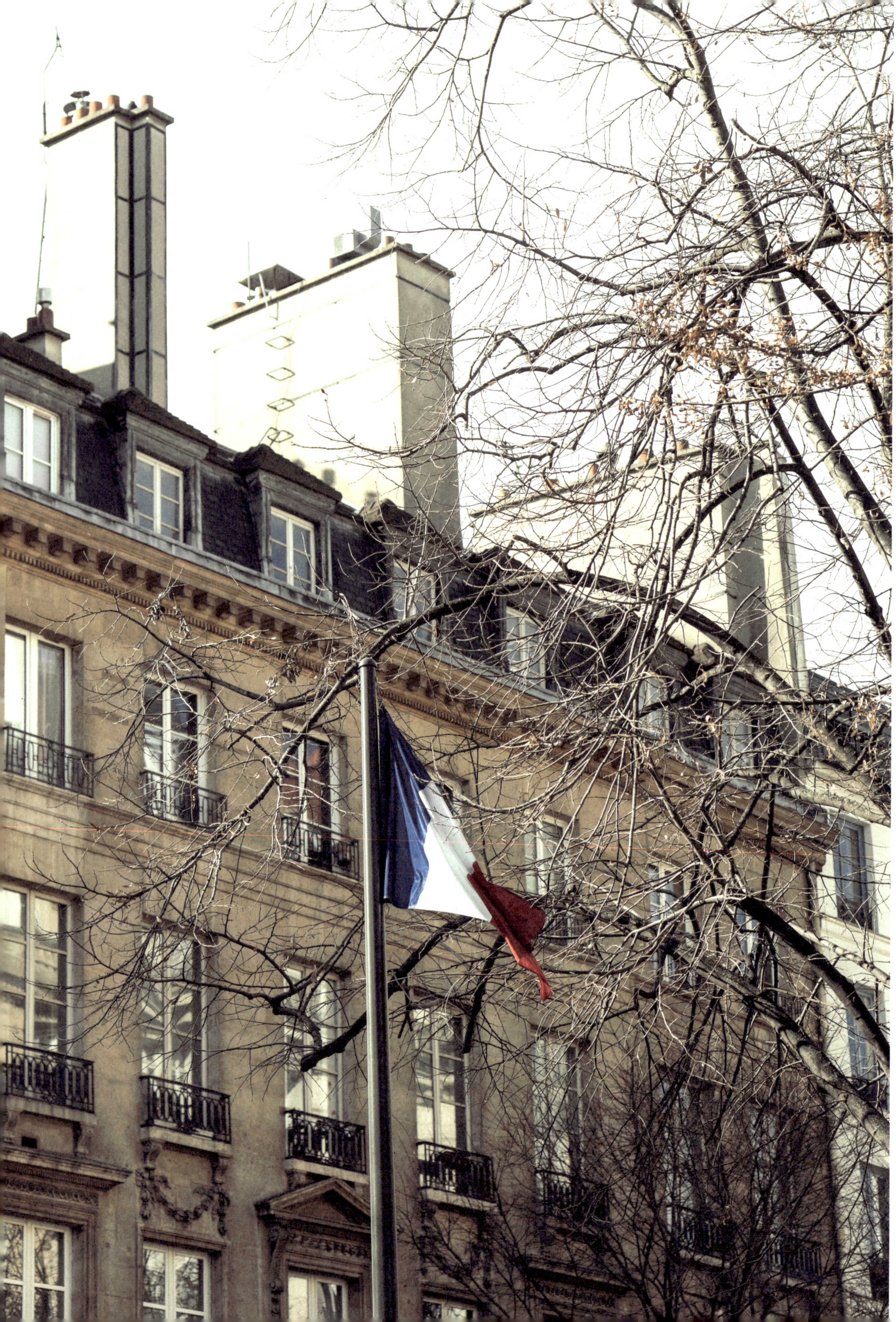

Heartbroken in Paris

WORDS
Laura Steiner

PHOTOGRAPHS
Augusta Sagnelli

My brain felt like it was still six hours behind on the other side of the Atlantic when I emerged at the Tuileries Métro station one early morning in April. I stepped out onto the street as one does from a heavy night of sleep: with crusty eyes and the slight confusion of whether or not what's in front is real or still part of the land of dreams. The sky was purple and Paris looked beautiful. I took the first right and a man standing against a jewelry storefront that was still closed greeted me with "*ça va?*" I had been inadvertently staring at his fingers while he rolled a cigarette. The dreaminess was gone: the man was real and so was my craving for a smoke. "*Ça va*," I responded, and in very broken French asked if I could have some tobacco and rolling paper.

A break up had occurred months before, but the ache still drove me to seek solace in cigarettes. The smallest things—a downpour, talking to a stranger, or hearing a song by The National—would make me feel sad almost on call. The beautiful morning light and my foggy, jetlagged brain, had the same effect too. The sun was starting to peek through the clouds when I put out my cigarette and said goodbye to the kind stranger.

I had nine hours in the city before having to ride back to the airport.

Musée de l'Orangerie opened its doors early, and Monet's "Water Lilies" brought back the gloomy feelings that the purple sky had triggered. But *ne pas fumer*—no smoking—inside the museum.

The museum was full of people: some speaking French, others broken French, and mostly people speaking other languages. There were tour groups, couples, and the occasional person visiting by themselves too. It was comforting to be in total anonymity, where I could disassociate myself from my own story. The possibility to exist as someone else for a day: a painter wanting to find some inspiration at a museum? A Parisienne who grew up coming to L'Orangerie? An unemployed writer spending their last pennies inside a museum? None of those characters had a broken heart.

I left the museum with the ghosts of possibility and a rumbling stomach. The next stop was a corner bistro, where I ordered buttery eggs and toast. Chairs with red upholstery lined the outside window, two to a round. It all looked very Parisian. The coffee tasted like a Parisian cliché too: bitter and burnt. It wasn't exactly tasty but it was a joy nonetheless, as if having terrible coffee, rollies, and the view of exquisitely dressed people running to work somehow put me in the same scenario I imagined so many writers had inhabited whilst crafting words from the City of Light. My mind went to grubby apartments with French windows and balconies with views of tin rooftops, to the 1920s, to decadence, to jazz.

I thought about Simone De Beauvoir; about James Baldwin's migration to Paris, and the subsequent work that came from that move; about Arthur Rimbaud's poems, and Patti Smith's obsession with Paris because of Rimbaud.

Back home in Bogotá, life happened in a swift way. Work and daily activities were urgent. And while I appreciated the lack of time to wallow too much, in Paris it felt as if the city had been expecting the slower pace of my melancholy.

And so for the first time in months, I wrote—a short piece inspired by the memory of the one I was missing:

RUE DE
TURENNE

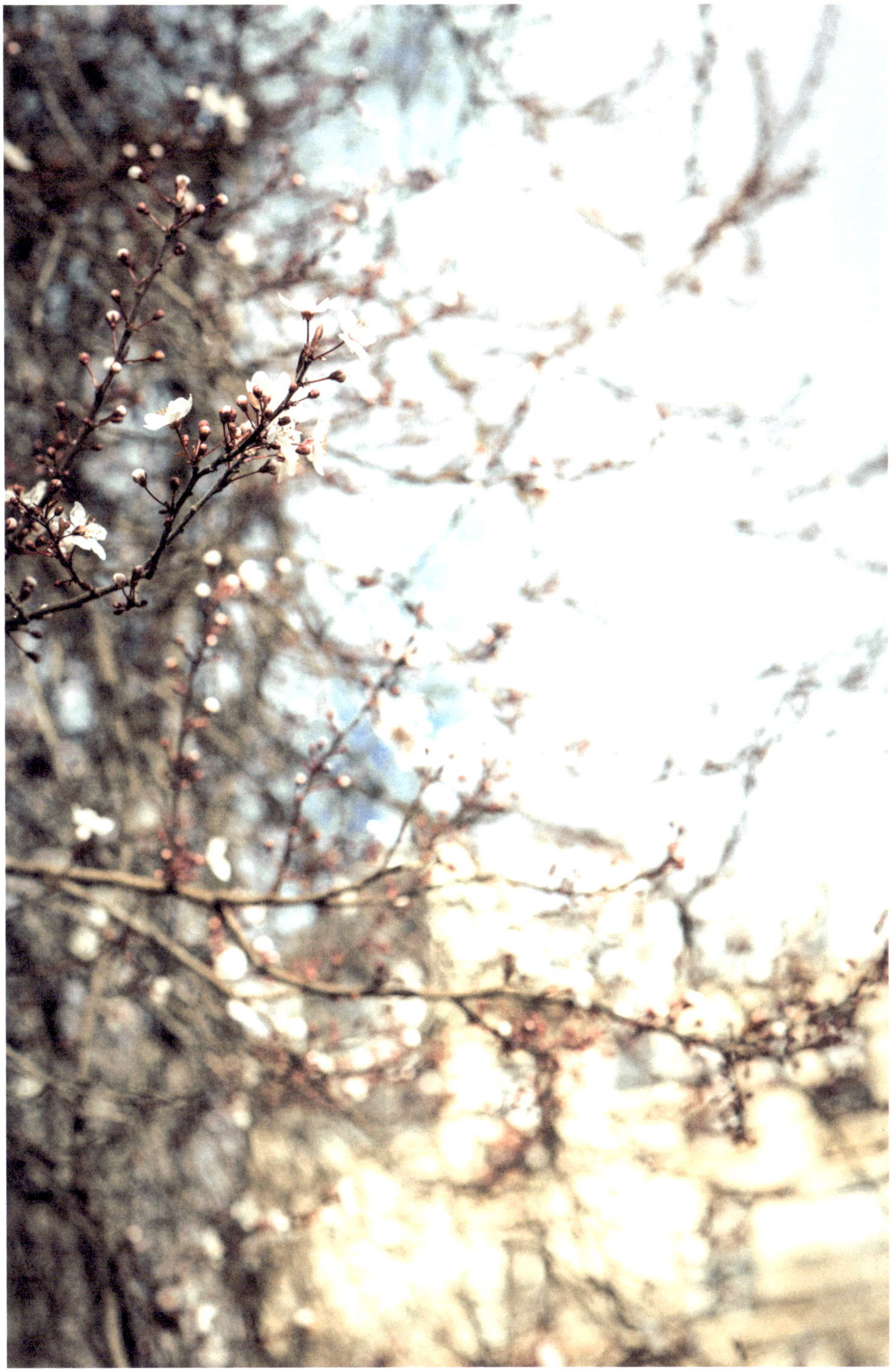

The Dancing Goat

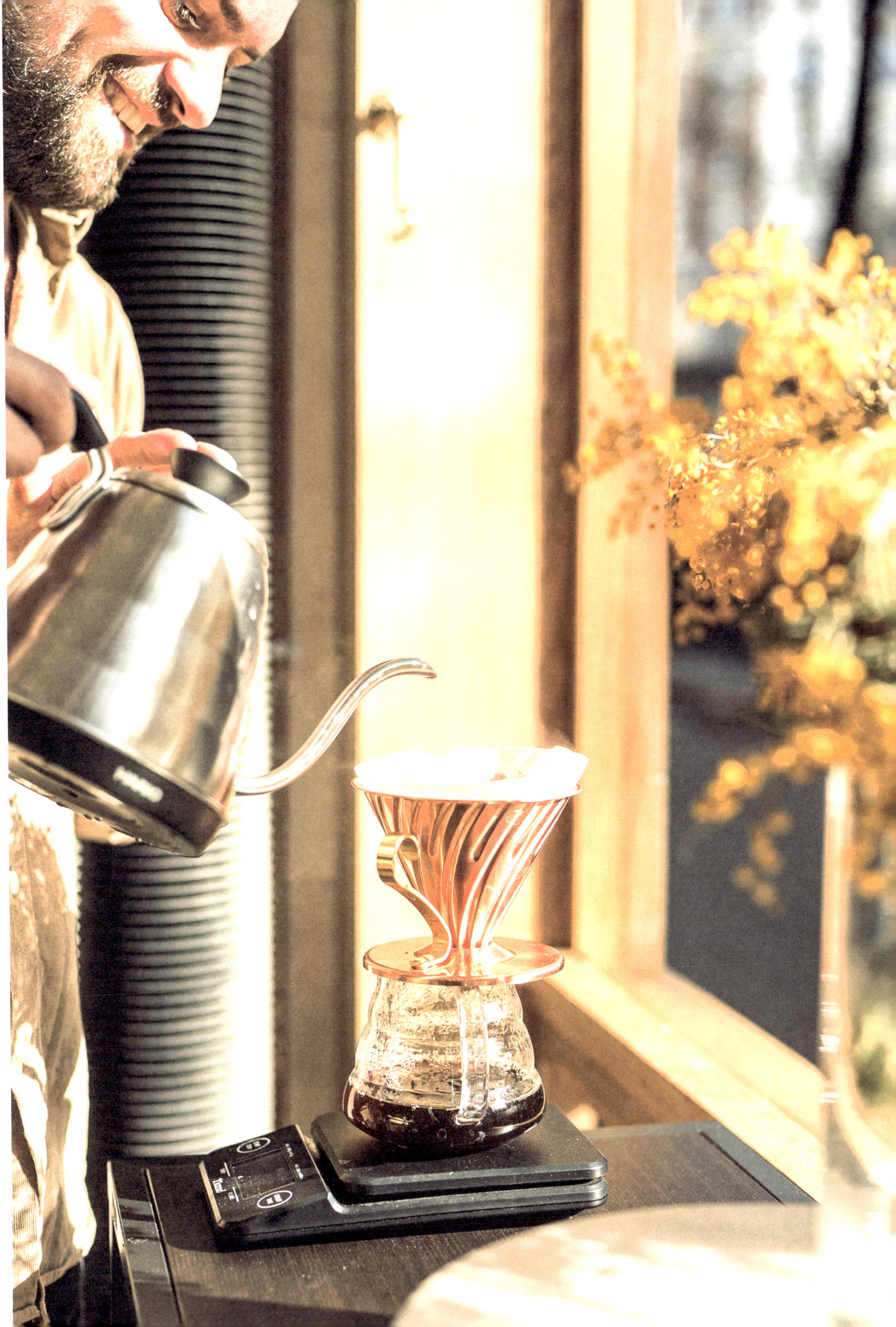

The Dancing Goat

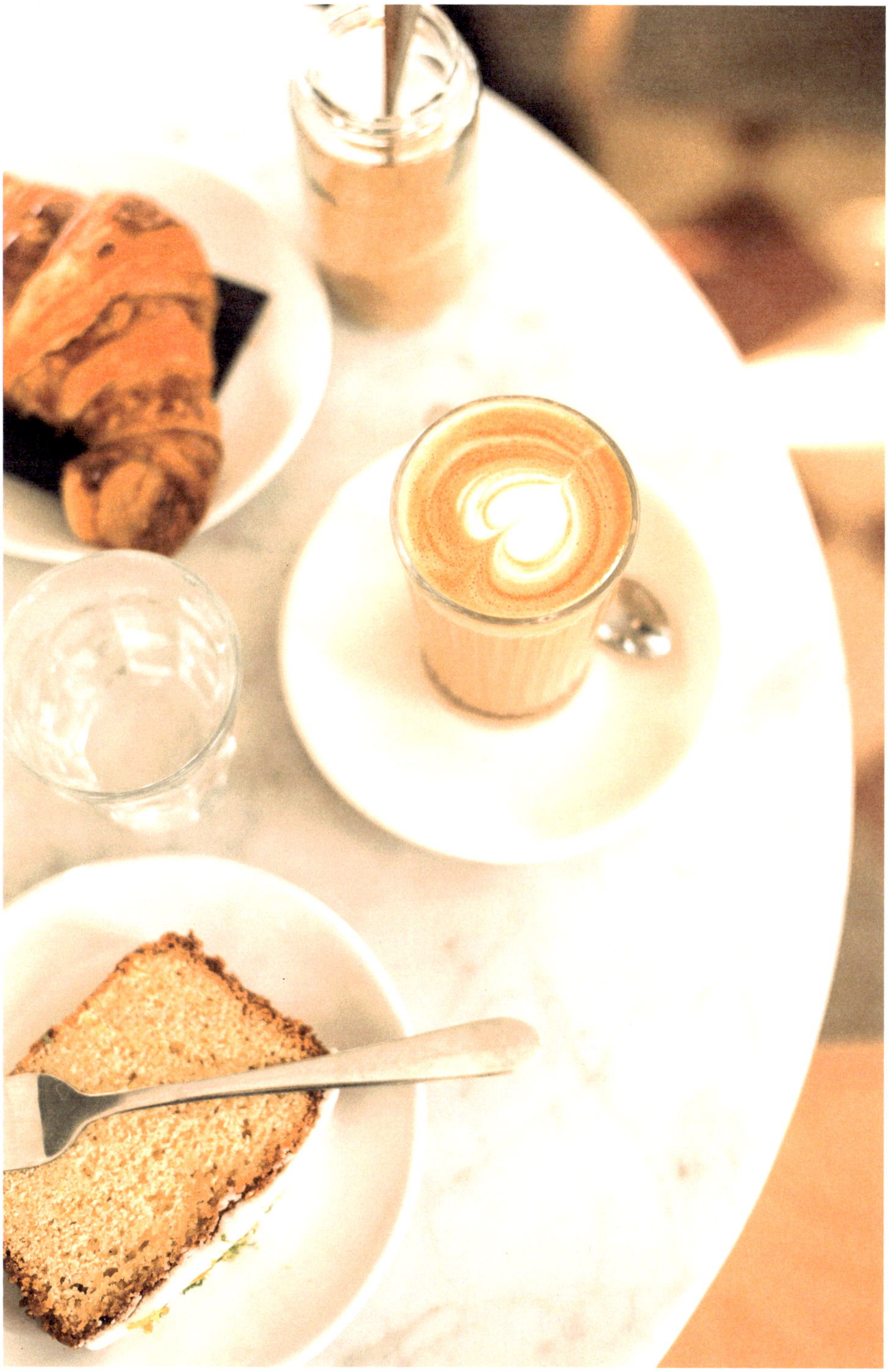

Fringe Coffee

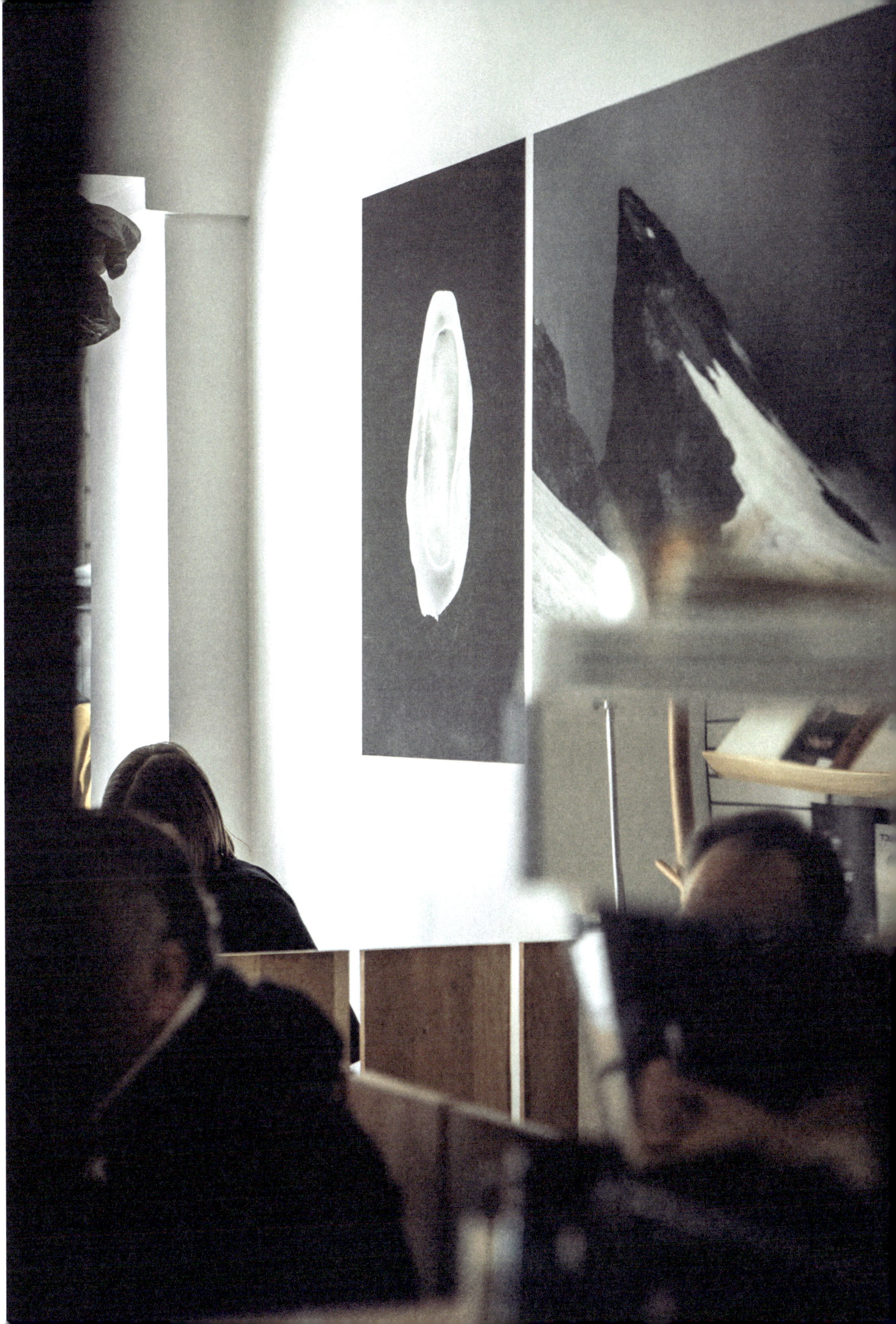

Fringe Coffee

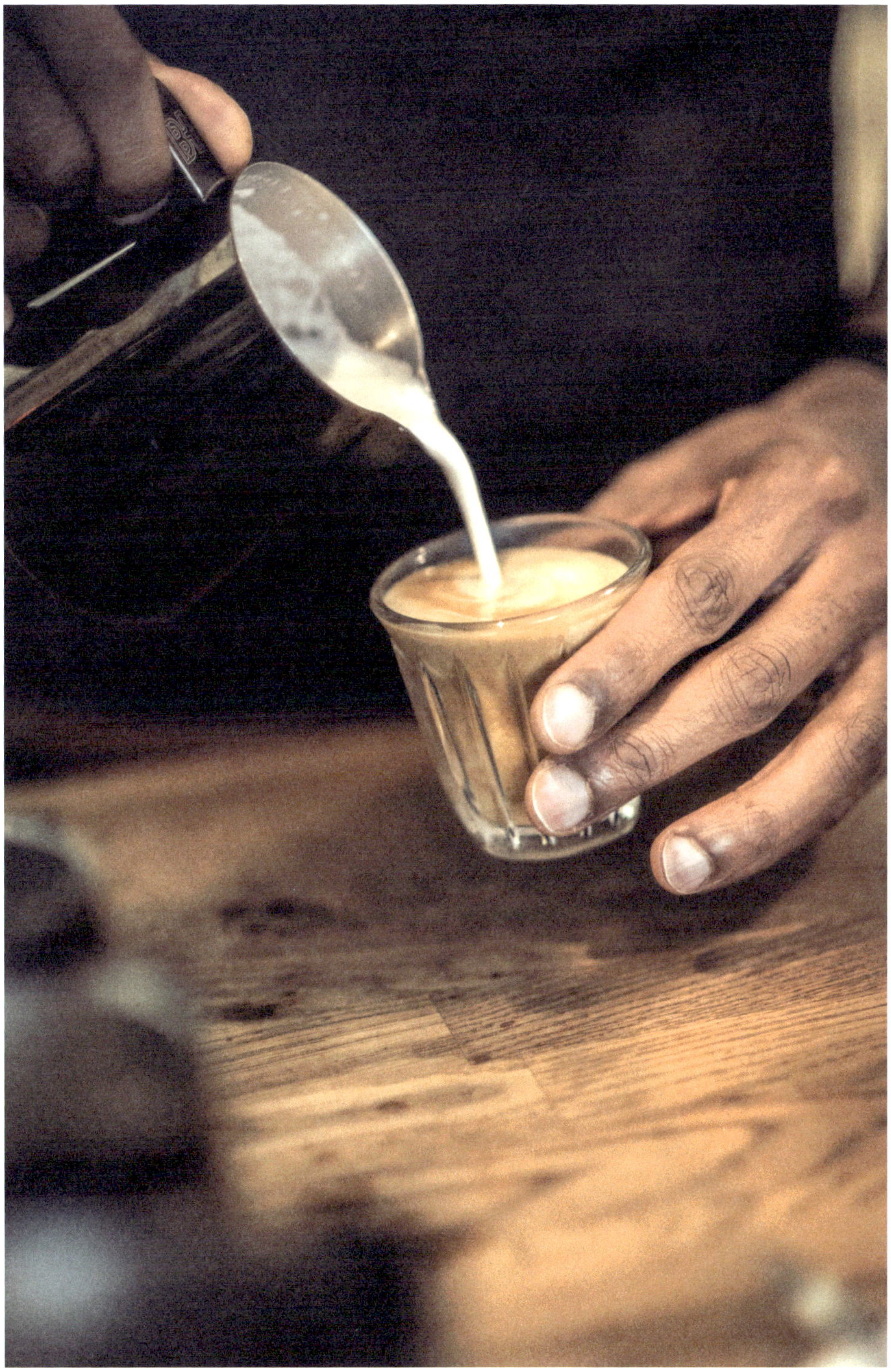

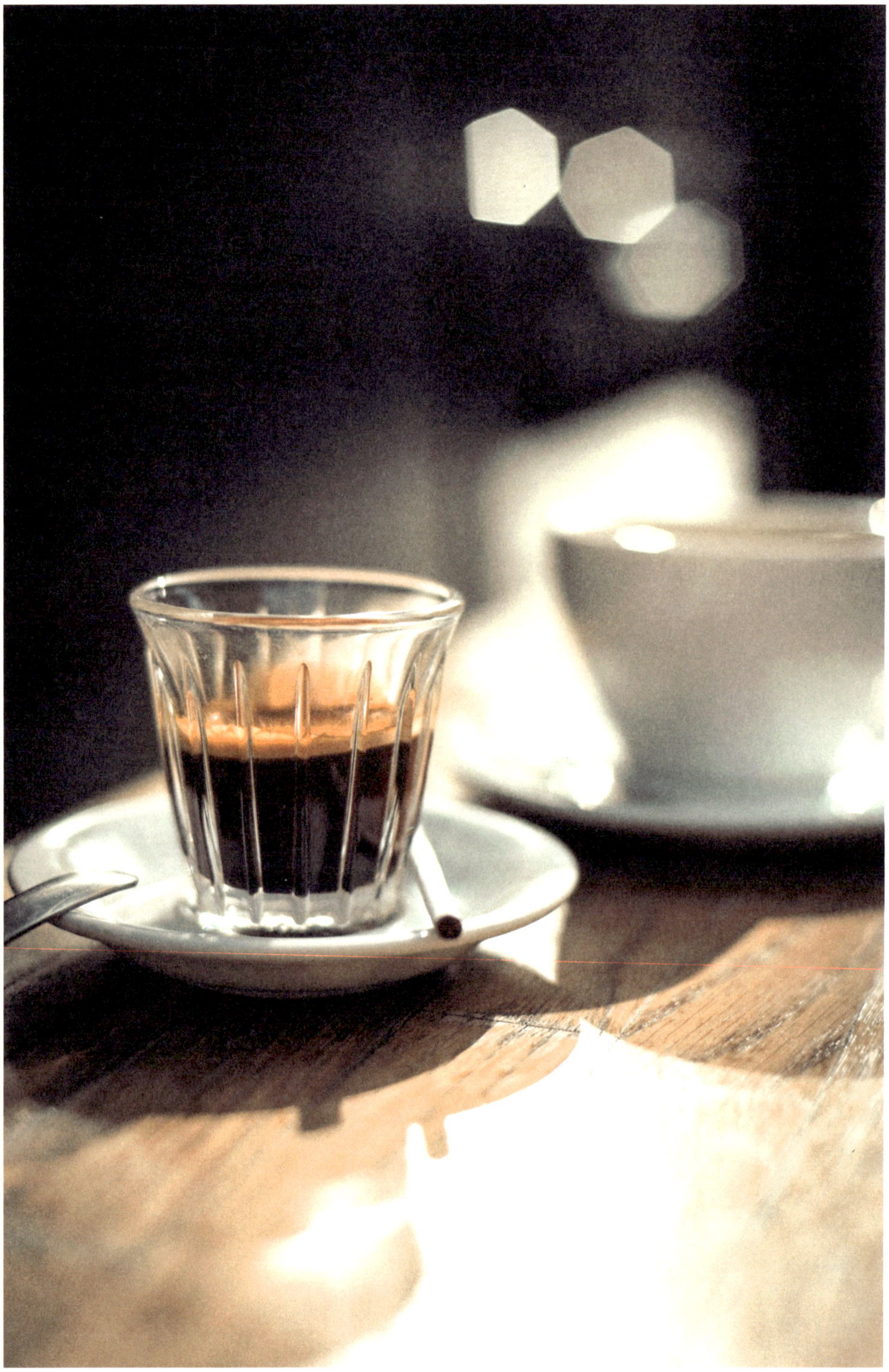

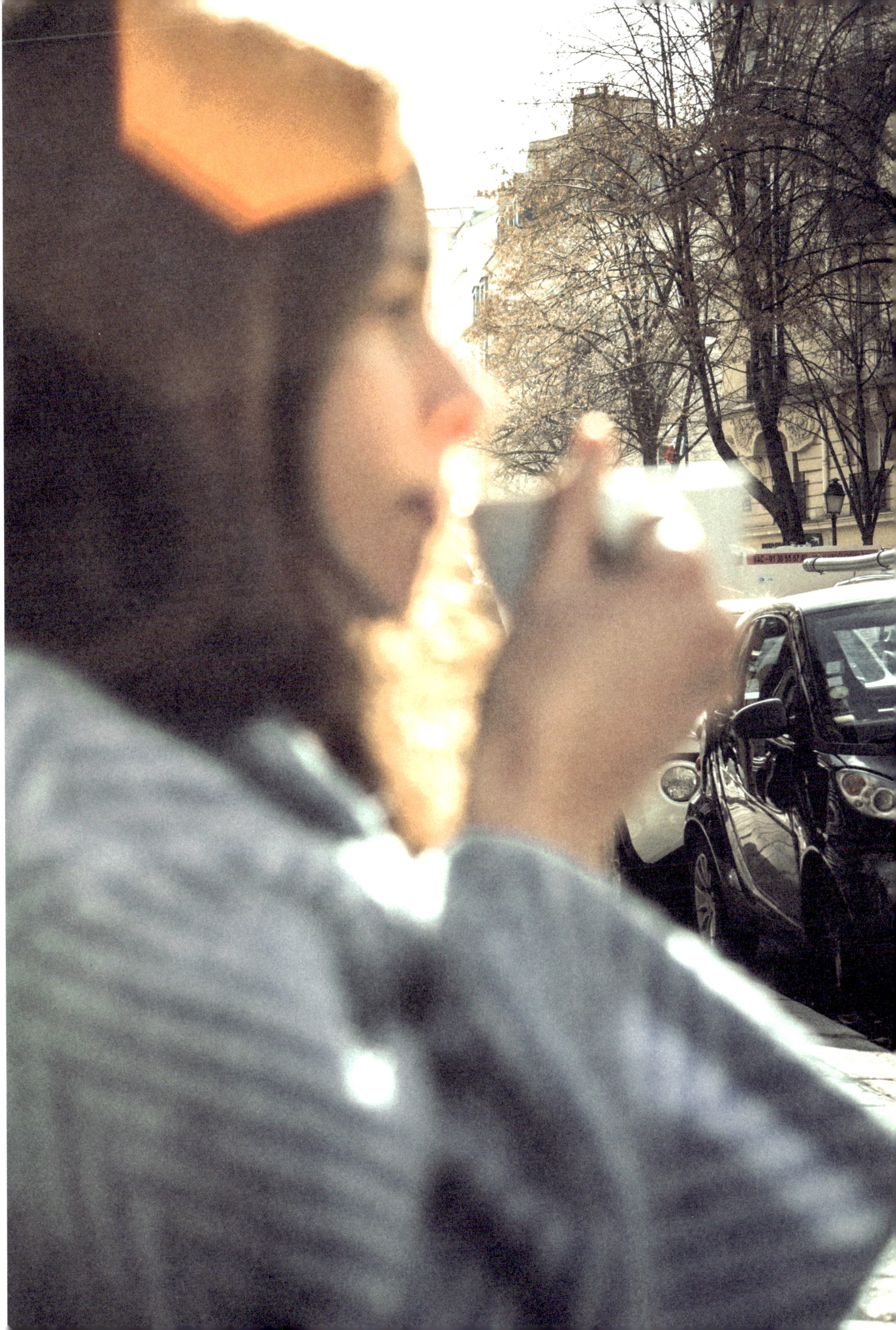

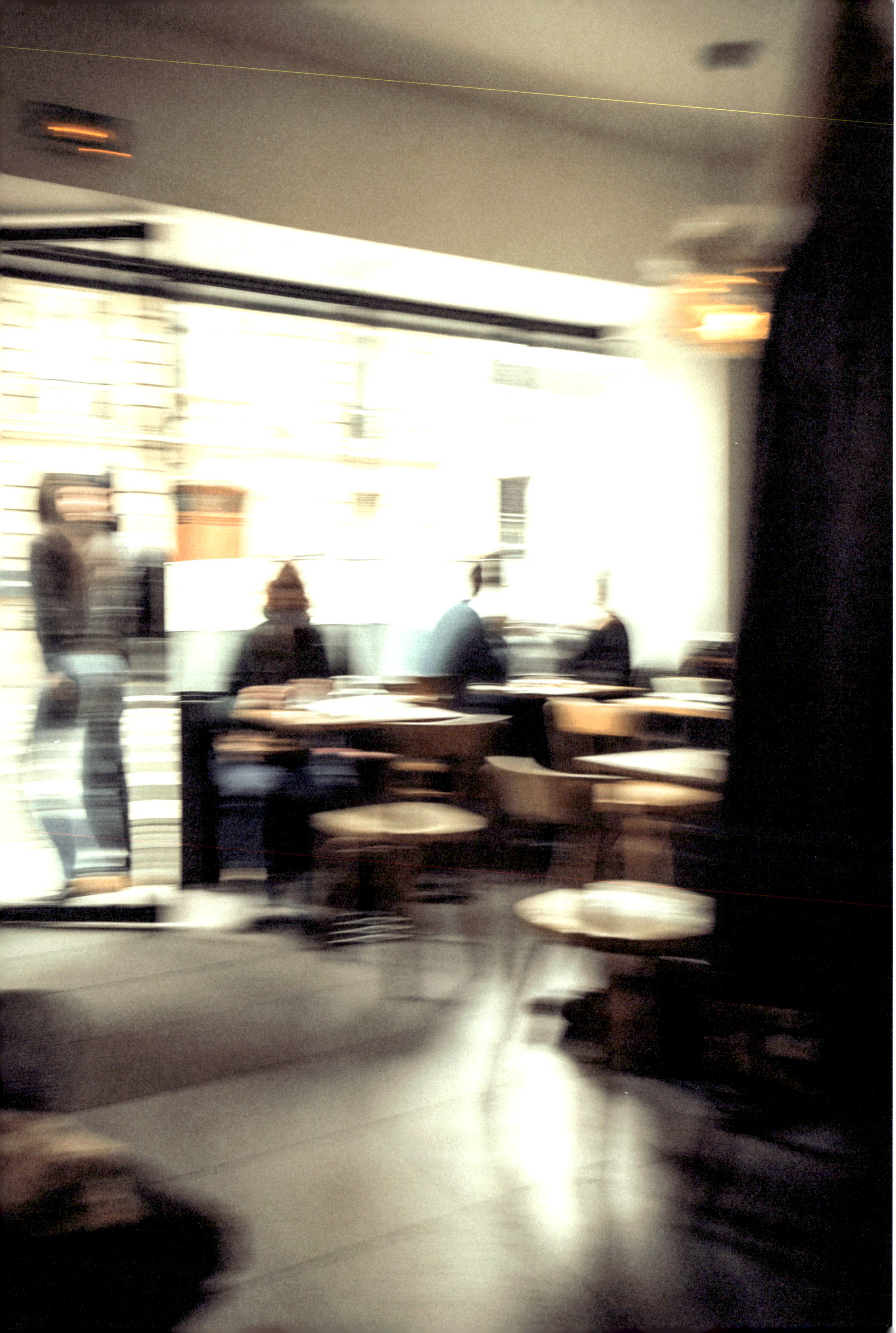

You pop into my mind in the City of Light. I guess Paris reminding me of you was bound to happen even though I've put you in the part of my brain that holds the things I've been losing track of. But a warmly lit corner of a French bistro with white brick walls, paper placemats and napkins with green stitching brings you to mind. An image of you half naked in a room where the walls are dark purple and there's a view of the Eiffel Tower. A perfect spring day in some other life. Maybe we should have come to Paris together more often.

In reality we hadn't been to Paris together. But whether we had, or we hadn't, it didn't really matter anymore because the heartbreak, as the relationship, was bound to become another story.

The ashtray filled and it was time to find better coffee. Less bitter. Hopefully unburnt.

Past the Centre Pompidou, across Le Marais, and into a fully awakened Paris with wine glasses clinking in the middle of lunch hour now, I stumbled into Fringe. The smell of freshly baked pastries was overpowering. It smelled of Paris. And more importantly it smelled of freshly made americanos. Just as thoughts of the Lost Generation of Paris had opened a well of writing that had been tightly sealed for the past few months, now the smell of perfectly brewed coffee asserted the joys of the simple pleasures in life.

On the wall hung photographs of different gradients of gray and blue. A photo of ice, of snow too, taken in Iceland by Icelandic photographer Ingibjörg Torfadóttir. Fringe was not the Paris of the 1920s but it was still Paris, with scrumptious art but better coffee and perfectly baked cardamom buns. It was still the Paris of people watching (the customer who took *all* of the chocolate cookies and ate two before he crossed the door on his way out), the Paris of love (I'm sure someone must've been making out in the booths), of art, of writers, of perfect sunrises that turn quickly into gray skies.

And for me, it was still the Paris of heartache and cigarettes.
—

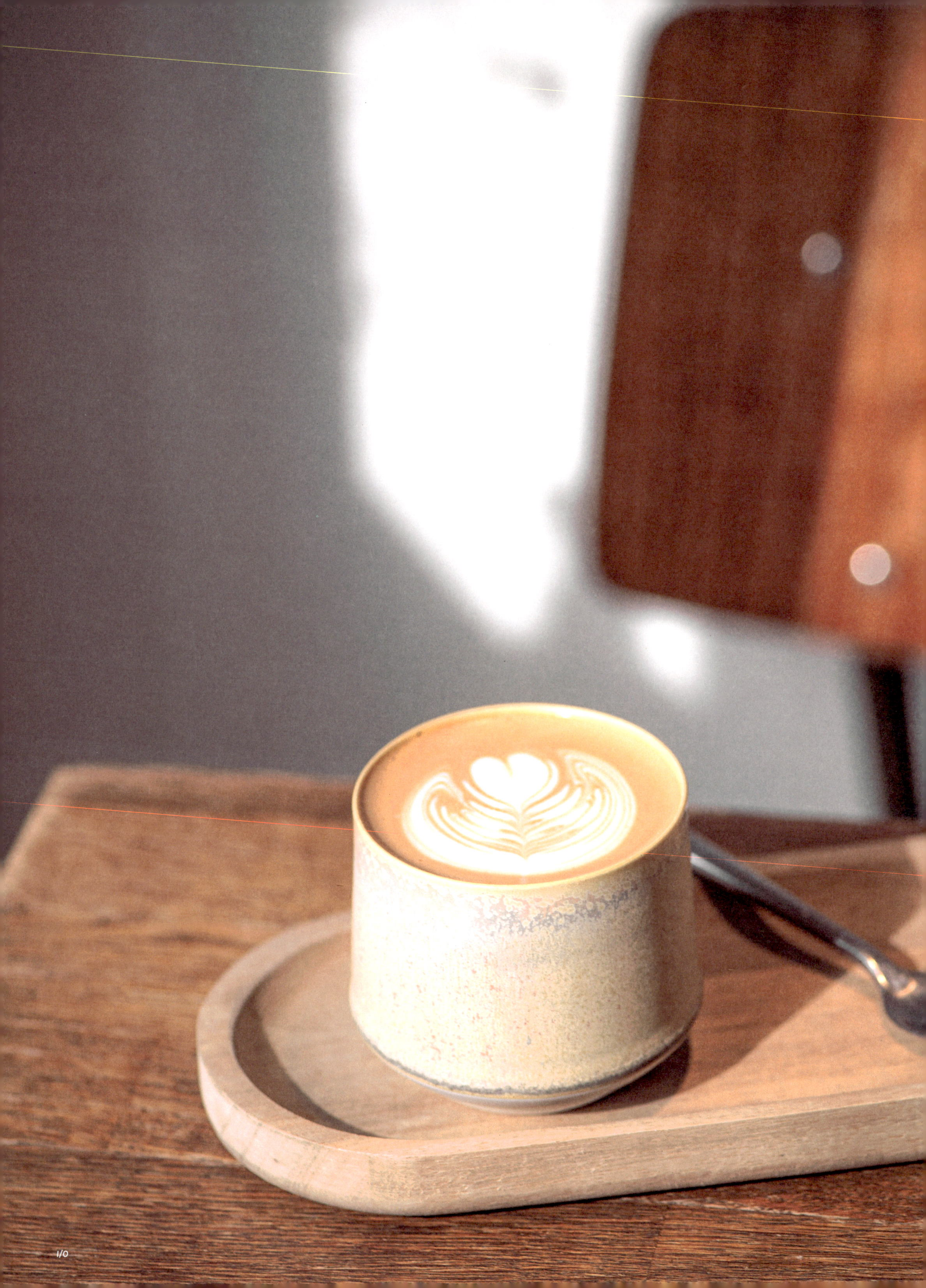

Flipping on the Lights

WORDS
Maggie Spicer

PHOTOGRAPHS
Antúria Castilho Viotto

"Please pull a single shot of washed Ethiopian for her." "This gentleman will take away his croissant." "She's going to reserve a ham sandwich for lunch." Co-founder Matthieu Meisse of I/O Café (pronounced "ee-oh"), a 3rd *arrondissement*-based coffee shop with a completely glass façade, calls out orders for a handful of regulars to one of his baristas on a Thursday morning.

I/O Café is a specialty coffee shop in the center of Paris, one of several that reflect an evolution in Parisian coffee culture that began just before the Covid-19 pandemic, and has continued throughout it. The cafe's name is cleverly taken from the universal "on/off" symbol, which is found on power switches of appliances, including the coffee bean grinder.

While there are standards in specialty coffee, such as the quality of beans that are sourced and best brewing practices, standards of service don't typically exist. What I noticed after a few visits to I/O Café is that I kept returning. And yet, it's not in my *arrondissement*. It's a detour.

"Let me open the door for you," continues Meisse that same morning. He proceeded to get the door for multiple customers, from a Monoprix grocery store clerk, to a smartly dressed gentleman visiting from Mexico.

In pandemic times especially, it makes a tangible difference to feel a sense of place, familiarity, and belonging. Being nestled in an artistic neighborhood filled with independent artists, a thought-provoking bookshop, and architects, I/O Café is surrounded by creative people. And, due to its approach to hospitality, it feels familial and welcoming, which is precisely the environment Meisse and co-founder Clement Hu were looking to create. "It's really a small village. We wanted regulars that were more than regulars—*habitués*—as we say in French. I think we managed to do that because our business is 70% regulars," explains Meisse.

These micro interactions prompted me to think about the dimensions of the specialty coffee movement. According to Wikipedia, "Specialty coffee is a term for the highest grade of coffee available, typically relating to the entire supply chain, using single-origin or single-estate coffee." Wouldn't these same standards extend to the quality of service within specialty coffee? Is it normal to expect a certain standard of service within a specialty coffee shop? Is it cultural? And is there a subculture within specialty coffee that's universal? Do I return mainly for the quality of coffee and textured milk, or for the way I feel interacting with the same barista visit after visit? Is it a combination of the two?

It certainly begs the question when one visits neighboring cafe Substance, located in a dark corridor along rue Dussoubs in Paris's 2nd *arrondissement*. Upon entering, one encounters a U-shaped bar, framing the flaming-red Slayer espresso machine, arguably the muse of owner and co-founder Joachim Morceau. Morceau sought to design the guest interaction with this open-plan, democratic approach to placing the coffee first, and to make it clear that you are there for the experience of coffee. Along those lines, Substance is famous for not offering sugar, *viennoiserie* (pastry), music, or non-dairy milks. It does, however, offer an on-brand bathroom, nonverbally yelling red-hued light the moment one swings open its door.

For many who patronize a coffee shop, the visit extends beyond the coffee—sometimes it's to share a conversation with a friend

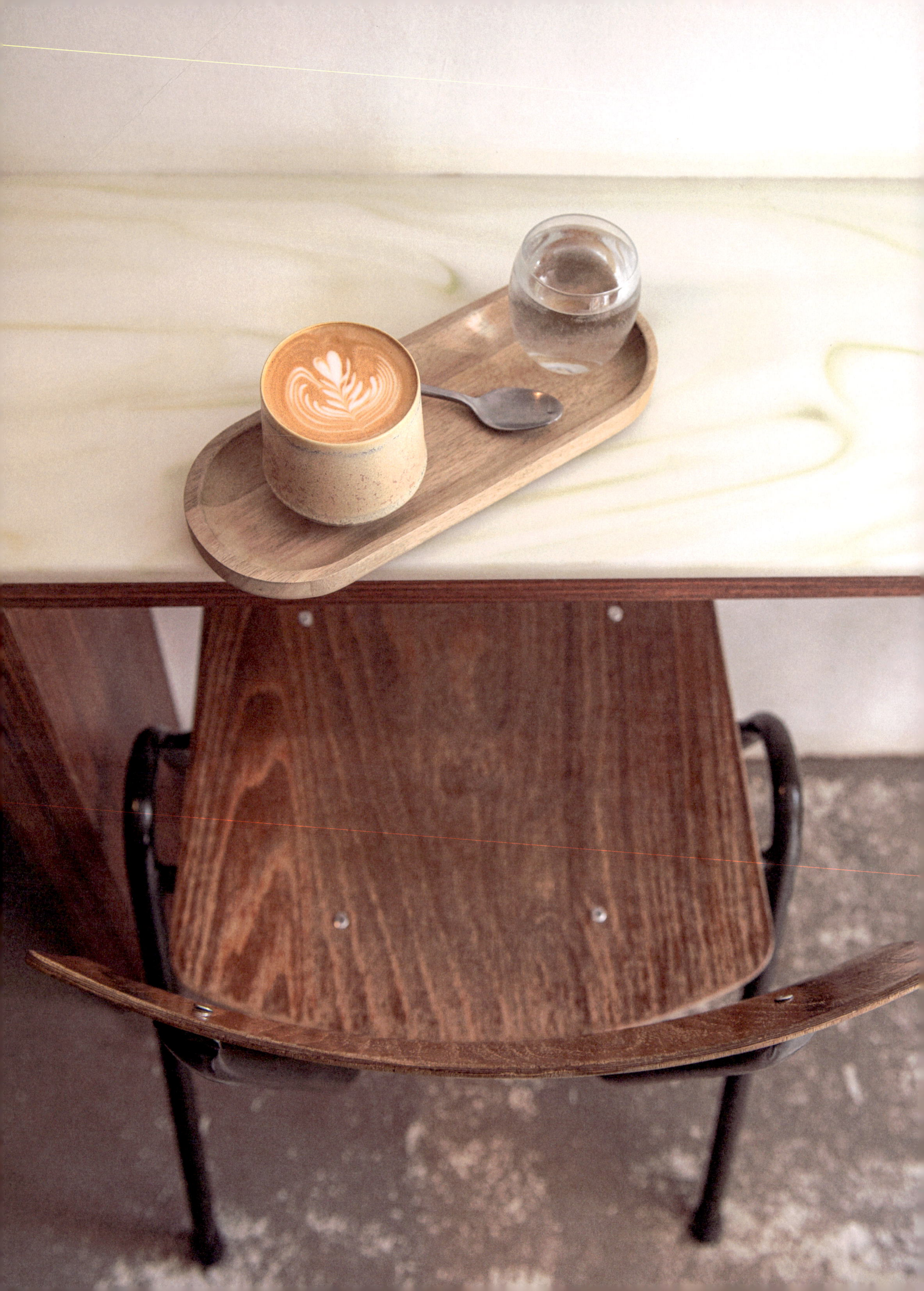

Leo Busnoult, I/O

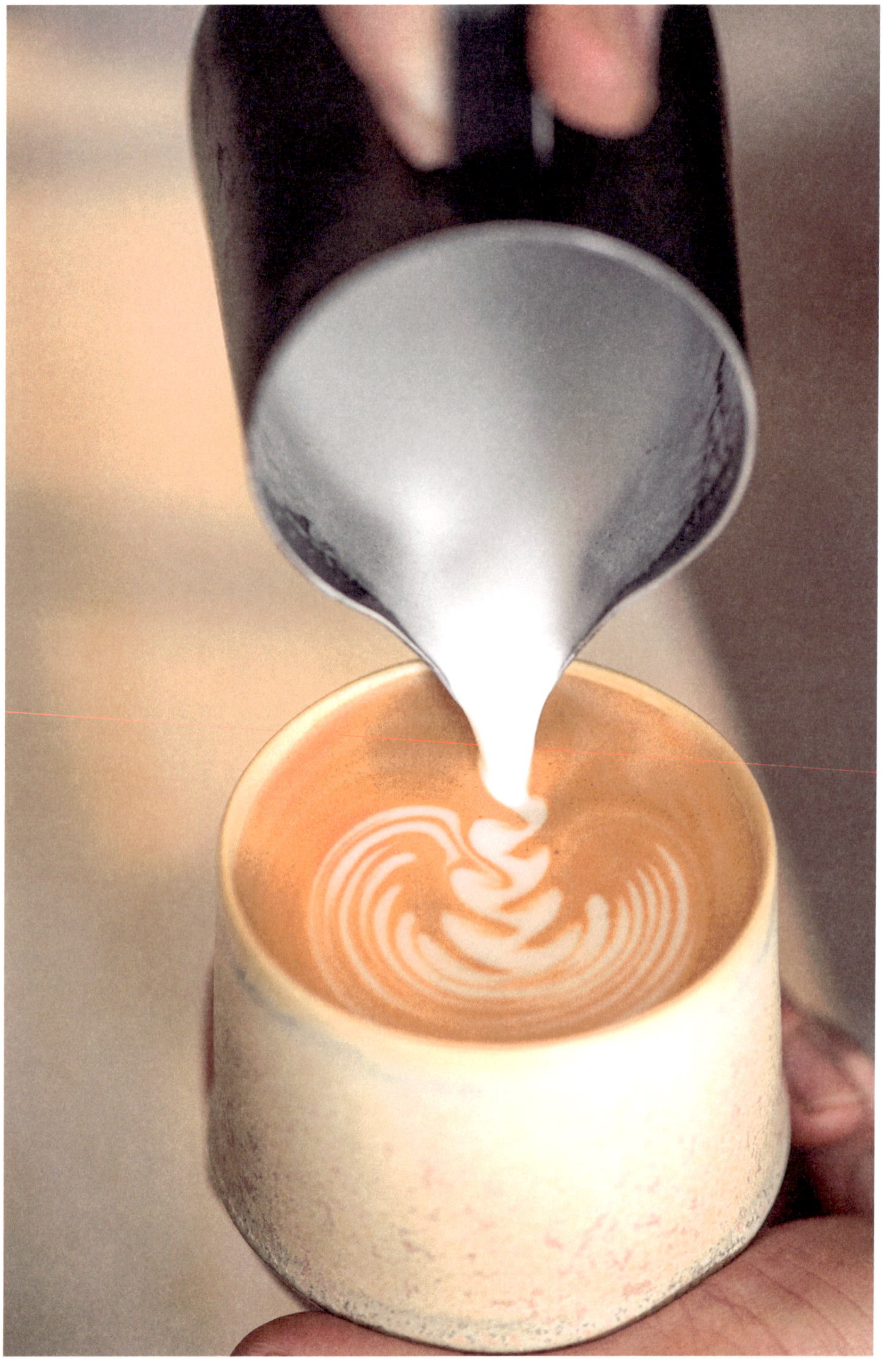

or colleague, other times it's to grab a quick energy boost, or perhaps it's the hour of *le goûter*, the French equivalent for a late afternoon snack. In fact, it's quite rare to find a coffee shop that caters specifically to the study of coffee. The closest equivalent would be attending a barista competition (coffee conference), which usually caters exclusively to the industry.

While for some it may feel stark to offer solely brewed coffee and espresso, it's an experience designed for the connoisseur. But, not dissimilar to the appreciation of wine, perhaps it's also a way to invite those curious but still on the fringes to venture inside the lab. "My shop is somewhere at the cross section of a barista championship stage, a theater, and a French bistro, where at times people speak together even if they don't know each other. Other times it's akin to a scene in a one-man show, like an omakase sushi bar. It draws upon multi-inspiration," shares Morceau. It's certainly the only place in Paris to get championship coffee.

And yet, both Morceau and Meisse share a belief in making coffee accessible while humbly extending an education and sincere hospitality. "I'm aiming to improve the coffee scene in Paris by bringing in renowned international roasters famous for their focus on high-quality coffee that emphasizes the relationship with the farmers, the beans, and terroir. I also highlight the role of water in coffee which I think hasn't been taken into consideration enough in France," says Meisse. "We use a different level of minerals for filter and espresso, for example. This is so important." Meisse wanted to introduce rare beans and varietals not previously available in Paris—Geisha, Sidra, Pacamara, Sudan, Rume, etc.

Paramount for him, though, is to offer excellent service. "This is really a weakness here in Paris. Parisian baristas can be quite arrogant because they think they know how to brew coffee, do a drawing on the latte—they are beyond saying hello to customers. That is something I strongly dislike," he laments. "Being polite, humble, and authentic in the way you serve your customers… this is the very, very, very first point." I/O Café offers a discount for Monoprix employees on the block. "Everyone is so dismissive of them. I feel it's really important to include them—it's not the coffee shop only for the trendy; it's also for the neighborhood. Whether a coffee geek or a 60 year-old woman, I want the customer to feel the same and for the coffee to be approachable," shares Meisse.

In many specialty cafes, baristas try to show off their coffee-making skills and the techniques that are required as a talented barista. "To me, what's more interesting is to speak about the coffee itself: where it comes from, the story behind it, the social interactions that are tied to the product. So rather than explain 'I'm using this machine, etc.' we focus on the coffee itself. Ninety-five percent of the work is done at the farm level. Like with wine, the sommelier doesn't speak about what he's doing table-side, but rather, he speaks to the type of grape, the region, and the soil where the grape is grown," continues Meisse. "It's one of many reasons we work with La Cabra, a roaster out of Århus, Denmark." Both the roaster and Meisse share similar values on a vision of coffee.

Like Meisse, Morceau prefers a lighter roasting style, one which highlights the terroir of the beans, not the flavors imparted from a darker roasting profile. "For me it's a little political. [Many] roasters have a darker roast to manage volatility in the beans and to not have to engage with customers. Light roasting necessitates more skills to brew a light roast correctly, and customers with a little more acumen," shares Morceau. Substance beans won't often have roasting flavors like caramel, for example. "They're going to be sweet, vegetal, floral, and fruity but rarely chocolatey because you don't taste chocolate or caramel when you eat a coffee cherry on the farm."

It's safe to suggest that offering more personal service and a lighter roasted bean together allow for more conversation between consumer and barista, a trend that, with I/O Café and Substance, one can expect to grow in Paris. "I see more specialty coffee shops opening here—in one year there have been Kitsuné, Kawa…within 500 meters you have five new places, and during a [pandemic] year no less. I hear of people living in London saying that the coffee scene in Paris is better because the quality of the black coffee has improved a lot." That's significant when one looks at Paris's historical adoption of more darkly roasted beans sourced from Italy.

Great hospitality, akin to the Japanese concept of *omotenashi*—or anticipating one's needs before they're spoken—is the foundation of an exceptional experience. Pair that with an honest espresso and you're guaranteed a refreshing experience.

—

Innovation Through Excavation

WORDS
Jae Lee

PHOTOGRAPHS
Fabian Schmid

"It is not difficult to design a new space in a historical building to show the juxtaposition of the old versus new. What we wanted to create was the continuity from the past to the future" says Paris-based, Japanese architect Tsuyoshi Tane of Atelier Tsuyoshi Tane Architects (ATTA). He recently completed a historic, monumental renovation of the Hôtel de la Marine, an 18th century structure on Place de la Concorde, which served as an office for managing the furniture of royal residences, including the Château de Versailles. The client, Sheikh Hamad of the Al Thani Qatari royal family, envisioned transforming the interior into a modern, 21st century-style museum. But Tane had a different design approach in mind, and in the end, Tane's solid belief in innovation through excavating past memories won Hamad over. "As we dug into the past of the site, we [discovered innovative ways to incorporate] historical ornamentations," Tane explains. "Rocaille decorative [elements] of the 1700s went extinct when Neoclassicism took over," says Tane. So he hung golden Rocaille-style ornaments from the ceiling of the Al Thani Collection's dimly lit entrance. Other features inspired from Tane's look back in history include parquet floors, in the style of the palace at Versailles.

One of the ATTA's early projects was Toraya Paris—a Japanese confectionary with over 450 years of history that serves tea. Toraya's philosophy of *wa* (harmony) turned it into an integral part of Japan's traditional tea ceremony. "We dug up the tradition of Toraya's craftsmanship, including [its] ancient recipes, using local and seasonal ingredients," he explains. "As we read through how Toraya creates the taste of *wa*, we decided to use local French materials such as wood, stone, stucco, or brass to present the harmony of time and space." For Tane, the challenge was digging up the past in France's tea culture.

"We were interested in the salon culture of France as well, where culture blossomed. This history has largely been replaced by corporate chains, which [poses a challenge to integrating] the past culture and art of tea that existed in both France and Japan," says Tane.

"Our idea of architecture is based on continuation instead of deviation, which is why I am deeply into the field of archeology. By digging through history, we can connect [with] the memory of a site, which results in surprising discoveries. And for me, that is sustainability."

Like Japan's tea ceremony houses, France's salon culture might have diminished. But there is an alternative way to experience France's history with tea from its herbalists, whose approach to tea is medicinal. They tailor bespoke teas or tinctures according to one's needs. One of the oldest *herboristeries*, offering custom tea since the 1800s, is the Herboristerie de la Place de Clichy. Located near the Museum of Romantic Life, its antique shelves are filled with bottles and sachets of hundreds of varieties of herbs.

As for the architect's daily coffee fix, he and his team members' favorite spot is a classic brasserie, Café Charbon. Opened in 1863, it's around the corner from Tane's brick, warehouse office, which was once occupied by the first manufacturer of meter sticks, founded after the Paris Meter Convention agreement was signed in 1875. "We have recently relocated [to a different space], so I'm searching for a new coffee spot, but as an architect, I was glad to have worked in a warehouse with such history. It is my personal preference but I recommend stopping by Café Charbon for a simple *allongé*. And for any mathematics or architecture enthusiasts visiting Paris, check out the brick warehouse."
—

Hôtel de la Marine, Place de la Concorde

Hôtel de la Marine

Toraya

Herboristerie de la Place de Clichy

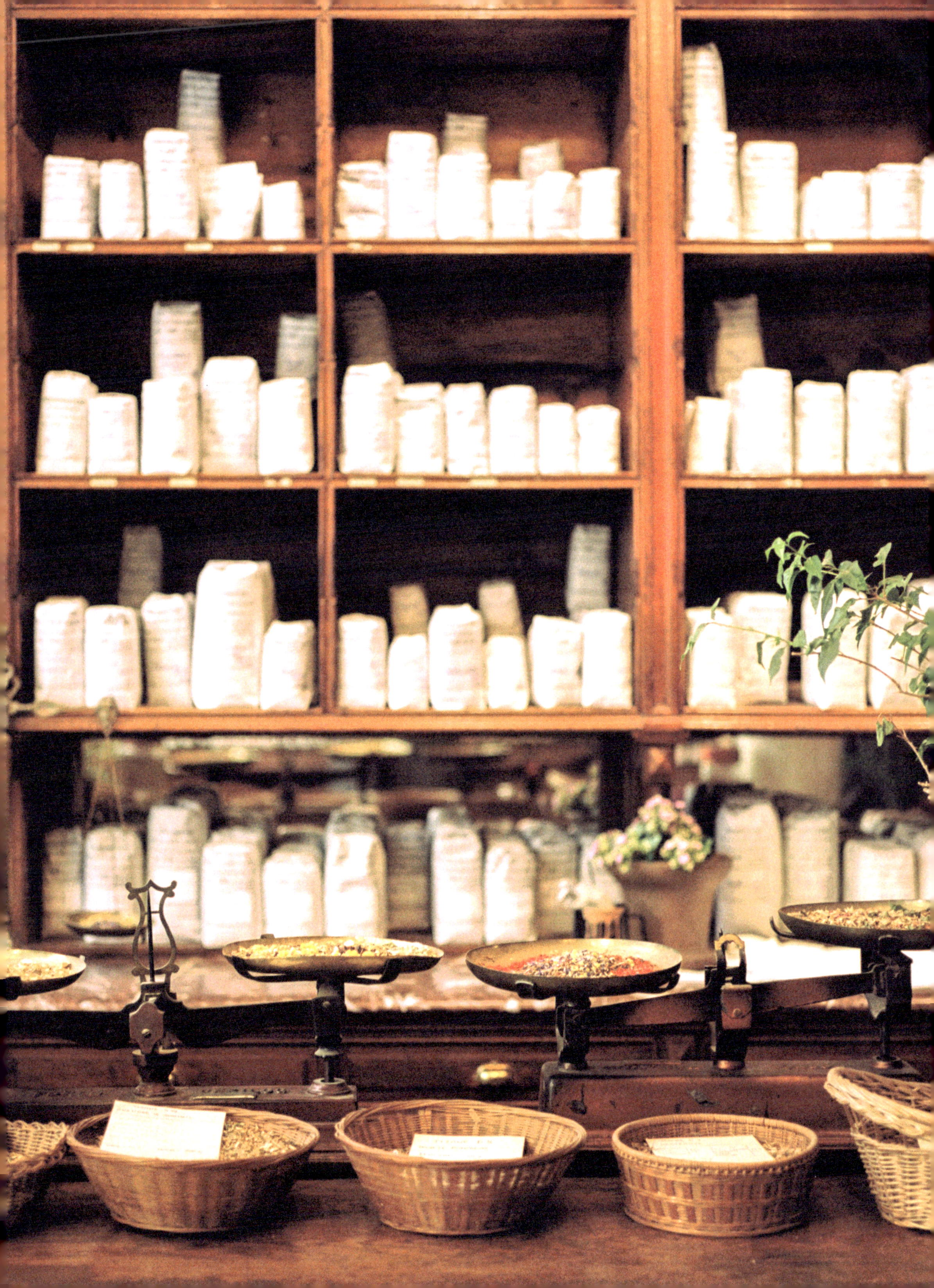

The Roots of Café Chicorée

WORDS
Shanthy Milne

POSTER
Courtesy of Leroux

"The truth seems to be, that Coffee is not what people call Coffee, unless a certain quantity of Chicory be prepared along with it; and it is rather remarkable that the world has been so long in getting at this fact."
—William Law, Coffee Merchant to the Queen of the United Kingdom, 1850.

Many writers and food historians have mused over the French predilection for strong, bitter-tasting coffee. Some have blamed the country's colonial endeavours for the nationwide dominance of the harsher-tasting Robusta bean, the caffeine content of which is almost double that of its smoother, more palatable Arabica cousin. Meanwhile, others have taken issue with the manner in which French coffee is prepared, berating the ill-fated combination of ultra-pasteurized milk and mediocre machines, often gifted to cafes by large coffee distributors in exchange for a commitment to serving their second-rate and often over-roasted beans.

Yet there has also been another, oddly commendable factor at play in the French acceptance of the Robusta bean. Whilst other nations strived to protect the purity of their coffee, the French did not shy away from experimenting with methods of adulterating the beverage to suit their needs. Indeed, it could be said that it was this very resourcefulness, which led to the French discovery of chicory as a coffee additive, that allowed the Robusta bean to remain prevalent in France for over three centuries.

In the 1800s, whilst the British Parliament was attempting to impose sanctions on domestic coffee dealers bold enough to cut their blends with factitious coffee substitutes (regardless of any positive impacts on flavor), France remained open to the possibilities such blending offered. Thus, the French discovered ingenious ways in which to make poor quality coffee palatable through the addition of home-grown additives. These not only enhanced the flavor of the coffee, but also reduced the price of the final coffee product and extended its availability and reach. In wartime, these additives even served as cheap, readily-available substitutes for the real thing.

The most notable of these additives was roasted chicory root, which became a French stalwart during the Napoleonic Wars and established itself as a gastronomic staple that continues to be enjoyed in French coffee to this day— albeit on a far smaller scale.

In his book "The History of Coffee, including a Chapter on Chicory," Scottish coffee merchant William Law praised the French use of chicory, stating, "The Chicory seems to give body to the Coffee. It gives it also depth of colour: but that is nothing. It fortifies the quality of thinness in the Coffee, imparts that softish and pleasing aroma which makes the beverage acceptable. Besides this, we are informed that Chicory improves the medical virtues of Coffee, by neutralising in some degree its constrictive effects."

In its purest form, this coffee concoction derived from the roots of the common chicory plant became known by the French as *café chicorée*. Outside of its use as a coffee additive, most of us will be familiar with the leaves of the chicory plant in their crisp and slightly bitter salad form. Other varieties of chicory, such as the Belgian witloof, are force grown in dark conditions and served as a delicacy in the Flanders region and also in the United States, which imports around $5 billion worth of witloof annually. Every part of the chicory plant has a recognized culinary and medicinal use, but it is the root, which contains high quantities of inulin (a type of dietary fiber and also a prebiotic that encourages the growth of healthy gut bacteria) for which it is most desirable. Chicory is in fact the primary source of inulin in modern-day supplements.

In France, the trend for chicory coffee reached its peak during the early 19th century as a result of Napoleon's continental blockade. After a series of military defeats by the British (particularly the Battle of Trafalgar, which decimated the French maritime fleet), Napoleon retaliated with a blockade preventing trade between continental Europe and the U.K. His intention was to damage Britain's economy, weakening the country sufficiently enough to allow him to launch

CHICORÉE LEROUX
CHICORÉE
EXTRA LEROUX
La Chicorée Leroux est la meilleure
d'après Firmin Bouisset
LEROUX
LA LITHOGRAPHIE PARISIENNE, ROBIN, DIR. PARIS

a successful attack. However, in reality it had little impact on the British who were easily able to circumnavigate the blockade. Instead, Napoleon's actions resulted in significant shortages in France, including coffee which could no longer reach French shores due to Napoleon's refusal to receive goods traveling through British ports. Reciprocal blockades imposed by the British also prevented France from accessing coffee supplies from its own colonies.

In order to meet the public demand for coffee (and to feed his own well-documented addiction), Napoleon promoted the mass cultivation of chicory root in Northern France. Alongside chicory, the French grew beets in order to derive a form of domestic sugar to sweeten their coffee in the absence of the previously imported sugar cane.

Aside from the reduction in labor intensity brought on by technological advancements, little has changed in the processing of chicory coffee since Napoleon's time. Once harvested, the chicory root is cut into strips—*cossettes*—which are dried. As with coffee, a master roaster is then enlisted to oversee the crucial process of roasting *cossettes*. It is down to the well-honed skills of this individual to determine through smell and color assessment when the chicory has reached optimal caramelization, ensuring maximum flavor, without burning them. Once cooled, the *cossettes* are crushed into a grain form, which can then be filtered like coffee or finely ground into a soluble powder.

Whilst Napoleon is to be credited for making chicory coffee a staple in French homes, it was the arrival of the World Wars that expanded chicory coffee consumption beyond France, making it commonplace throughout Western Europe. During WWI, when enemy blockades cut off their supplies, the Germans were forced to create an *ersatz* coffee blend of roasted acorns, beechnuts, and chicory. Similarly, in WWII, rations and shortages meant that most households in Western Europe became familiar with chicory coffee in one form or other.

For this reason, whilst most Parisian natives, who have been converted by the virtues of a freshly ground, single-origin coffee, will likely turn their nose up at a mug of *café chicorée*, it's likely they will harbor fond recollections of their grandparent's generation enjoying the beverage as part of their at-home, breakfast routine. Though the tradition of drinking *café chicorée* was not passed on to subsequent generations, the taste for chicory coffee did spread to other parts of the world, where the tradition has held strong.

Echoing the birth of chicory coffee in France, in America, the French-founded city of New Orleans also developed a love for chicory as a result of military blockades—this time during the American Civil War. But in New Orleans, once the practice of mixing chicory with coffee had begun, it became firmly ingrained in local culture. Even today, it remains a local speciality and few tourists will leave New Orleans without enjoying the famous combination of a chicory-laced *café au lait* served alongside a beignet (a French-style doughnut). In New Orleans, the speciality is not exclusive to people's homes and can still be enjoyed in cafes, the most notable of which is the landmark Café du Monde, which has been serving chicory coffee since 1862.

Most of the chicory used in New Orleans coffee is still sourced from Northern France. Though production is significantly less than during the Napoleonic Wars, some of the key production facilities have survived. The most famous of these being Leroux (founded in 1858), a household brand in France that is so firmly established in the French psyche that it's home city of Orchies is now synonymous with chicory production.

Leroux claims that when blended with a ratio of ¼ chicory to ¾ coffee, their chicory will reduce the caffeine content of your coffee and soften its taste, imbuing it with a deliciously light caramel flavor, perfect for enhancing the taste of a standard household coffee.

As early as 1885, even the British had to concede that this blending did in fact make for a superior coffee. Giving evidence to a Parliamentary Committee on Adulteration, a representative from the Inland Revenue admitted: "The trade contend that good coffee, mixed with one-eight part of chicory, and sold at a moderate price, makes a better beverage than ordinary coffee would do at the same price, and the great mass of the public prefer it."

Whilst historic companies such as Leroux continue to dominate the chicory market in France, in the Netherlands a much smaller, self-proclaimed "hipster" company has also tapped into the benefits of chicory. According to David Klingen, one of the company's founders, its organic chicory coffee product Chikko Not Coffee is primarily aimed at what the marketing world describes as "dark green customers"—namely, those who make their purchase decisions based on environmental factors.

Klingen compares chicory to tofu, in that tofu might be used by some as a meat substitute but it can never truly replicate or replace meat. In the same respect, although chicory can achieve a 60% likeness to coffee, he admits that a complete likeness is impossible.

For Klingen, this is one of three factors that limits the popularity of chicory coffee. The absence of caffeine is another. Whilst some health-conscious customers actively seek out caffeine-free options, Klingen claims the majority of coffee-lovers find the absence of caffeine a deterrent. Finally, as it is primarily consumed as an instant drink, chicory coffee cannot mimic the rituals of coffee preparation, a crucial factor preventing chicory from being a real challenger to coffee.

Perhaps Klingen is unconventionally honest about the limitations of his own chicory product because he is about to launch a new coffee substitute, which he claims will address these limitations. His new product Northern Wonder has already achieved an 80% likeness to coffee and he believes there is potential to achieve a 100% likeness in the future.

The driving force being the company is a commitment to reducing the rate of deforestation being caused by coffee production. A recent WWF (World Wildlife Fund) study ranked coffee as the 6th largest contributor to deforestation, a problem which is being exacerbated by increasing demand—particularly from traditionally tea-drinking nations like China and India. Climate change is also playing a role, shifting existing coffee growing areas away from their traditional highland habitats. With up to 80% of the now suitable land for coffee production being tree-covered, there is little chance of achieving the shift without further deforestation.

In response to these issues, Northern Wonder has been entirely created from non-tropical ingredients; a (currently secret) blend of roots, nuts, and seeds. Crucially, it also contains synthetic caffeine to provide that much needed hit. With the exception of being able to grind your own beans, the granular product promises to replicate all the other rituals of coffee preparation such as filtration, or even extraction via a coffee machine.

Recognizing that our demand for coffee has outstripped our ability to sustainably source it, Seattle based start-up Atomo Coffee was also founded upon sustainability-driven goals. Its molecular coffee substitute, launched last year, also contains caffeine and allows for the ritual of traditional coffee preparation. Like Northern Wonder, Atomo was very secretive about their recipe prior to the product's launch, stating only that its coffee would be derived from naturally sustainable, upcycled plant waste. When customers finally received the first shipments of Atomo last year, the ingredients were revealed to be: water, extracts of date seed, grape skin, inulin, natural flavors, caffeine, and unsurprisingly, *chicory root*.

A short distance away from the home of Leroux, celebrated French chef Florent Ladeyn has also embraced chicory as part of his mission for sustainable gastronomy. The former Top Chef finalist is now a proprietor of three hugely successful restaurants, including the Auberge du Vert Mont in Boeschepe, which enjoyed Michelin star status from 2013 through to 2019. Ladeyn's restaurants are characterized by locavore cuisine, with 99.5% of his produce sourced within a 50km radius. The only exception to this is salt, though even that does not travel far, coming from a small, one-man producer in Cap Gris-Nez. A menu without pepper, spices, olive oil, lemon, chocolate, and of course coffee, demands that Ladeyn be inventive. To replace the traditional and much anticipated after-dinner coffee, Ladeyn has crafted his own chicory blend in which the chicory is complemented by roasted sunflower seeds for a touch of fattiness and malt barley to balance the aromas. The steaming beverage is served in a filter coffee maker, recreating the ritual familiarity one associates with coffee.

Unquestionably, the increasing limitations on sustainable coffee production are reviving the demand for coffee alternatives and evidently, chicory still has a crucial role to play in this field. Few other natural products can replicate the flavors of coffee so readily. Though factitious coffee blends will likely require additional ingredients to achieve the ultimate goal of replicating true coffee likeness, it seems unlikely such a goal will ever be realized without chicory featuring as an essential component.

—

Finding Love at Shakespeare and Company

WORDS
Eve Hill-Agnus

PHOTOGRAPHS
Carlotta Cardana

The history of my life in Paris has always been intimately, inextricably, and irrevocably intertwined with the famous bookstore Shakespeare and Company. You could call it the meet cute of a lifetime: my mother American, my father Parisian, met at the English-language haunt that hugs the Rive Gauche, on the border of the Latin Quarter.

When they met, Shakespeare and Company was not the long-standing tourist lure it is now. But already, the shop was far from merely a shop. More than two decades before, in 1951, George Whitman had founded the literary enclave at 37 rue de la Bûcherie, having arrived in Paris just three years before.

An eccentric who wore paisley velvet jackets and satin shirts, Whitman entertained the most left-leaning political persuasions of the time and made the shop, with its green-painted façade, a haven for expats and bohemians alike.

As if echoing Mark Twain's satirical novel about American travelers, Whitman gathered "the innocents abroad." Like a bookish version of the Statue of Liberty, he welcomed the huddled masses to his literary shore.

Over the years, the likes of Anaïs Nin, Lawrence Ferlinghetti, Langston Hughes, and Richard Wright descended on the space, squeezing themselves into the nooks and crannies. The Beat writers of the 1950s, such as Allen Ginsburg, did readings there too—creating a version of Ferlinghetti's San Francisco bookstore City Lights for the City of Light. Upstairs, rooms held cot-like couches that turned into beds for the tumbleweeds who sought shelter for a night or a week in the "library," slipping upstairs with Whitman's permission after customers left.

Shakespeare and Company

148 — PARIS

Chris Jowitt, Shakespeare and Company

My parents met in the spring of 1976. The cheeriness of cherry season had arrived in Paris, but for my mother, it was a bleak, lovesick day. She had just broken up with her German fiancé and had been wandering the Boulevard Saint-Germain, weeping through the Latin Quarter in a mid-length skirt and boots. Drawn to Shakespeare and Company, where she knew she would find solace among the pages that tethered her to her faraway home, she entered the labyrinth of tiny rooms downstairs. Light was slanting in from the afternoon sun. Already, she was feeling better.

Among the tomes piled pell-mell and stacks askew, her eyes landed on a copy of William Shakespeare's "Henry V." It was exactly the title my father was seeking when he, too, entered the shop that afternoon—he was going to see the play that night at the Odéon theater, put on by the Royal Shakespeare Company.

Their fortuitous meeting at the bookstore progressed to a nearby cafe, where they shared a beer. And so their story went—one of just many authored among those stacks on rue de la Bûcherie. Upstairs, a wall displays notes and postcards from many who can say, like I can, that their existence is fundamentally tied to the bookstore that Whitman created.

Years later, in the wake of Whitman's death at age 98, his daughter Sylvia Whitman (who is almost exactly my age) and her partner David Delannet opened the coffee shop the white-bearded literary giant had always wanted.

In 2015, their cafe filled in the old bones of a derelict mechanic's shop next door to the bookstore, which had been left empty for years. The original 1970s mosaic tiled floor is juxtaposed with rough, stone walls. The tracks of sliding garage doors hold shelves in airy limbo. On a sunny day, you can sit on the cafe's terrace under warm rays, just beyond the shadow of Notre-Dame Cathedral.

One of the early third wave coffee shops in Paris, it boasts beans from Lomi, a roaster based in the Goutte d'Or neighborhood of the 18th *arrondissement*, and the bagels and pastries come from Bob's Bake Shop, owned by a native New Yorker.

During the pandemic's early lockdown, when Parisians were only allowed to circulate within one kilometer of their apartments, Shakespeare and Company's coffee shop mostly saw its Parisian neighbors. But now that travel, which was halted by the Covid-19 pandemic, has fitfully resumed, expats and natives mingle there again. And once more, the coffee shop is there for the aficionado of golden lattes and pies, or the *flâneur*, or for future Franco-American lovers like my parents—she a heartbroken singleton, he a theatrical hopeful, serendipitously united, against all odds, in the company of Shakespeare.

—

PARIS — 151

Xavier de Parseval & David Elbaz, Le Cafe Gagnant

A Winning Change

WORDS
Anna Richards

PHOTOGRAPHS
Sujin Kim

The bright yellow tricycle is the only splash of color on a wet day in Paris. Rain slicks the cobbles of the courtyard, puddling between the stones and steaming up the glasses of the smiling young men behind the tricycle: proprietor Xavier de Parseval and trainee David Elbaz. David hands me an oat milk latte, flower petals carefully crafted in froth, and I clasp my chilly hands around the cup. The rich aroma is one of promise: this cup of coffee is set to change lives.

Le Café Gagnant, 'the winning coffee,' is an ambitious new project that aims to get Paris's homeless off the streets by training them as baristas to help them to find full-time employment. The three young visionaries who started the project are barely older than their first trainee. De Parseval met his co-founders Benjamin Salem and Jennifer Baleon in engineering school when they were all in their twenties. It has been an uphill battle to start such an innovative project during a pandemic, but together—Ben, Jen, and Xav, as they're known to friends—greeted each hurdle with energy and enthusiasm.

The project was born on holiday. Ben and Jen, who have been together for nine years now, were visiting London when they stumbled across the company Change Please, a social enterprise that reinvests 100% of its profits into training people, who are experiencing homelessness, with barista skills and providing them with a living wage. They couldn't understand why something similar didn't exist in their hometown.

A little research revealed that 80% of Parisians drink coffee daily. This was hardly a surprise, given that this was the city of Voltaire, who reportedly drank up to 50 cups of coffee a day. On a somber note, they also discovered that Paris has the highest rates of homelessness in the country. With approximately 30,000 rough sleepers, Paris accounts for 44% of homelessness in France. Amongst these, only a quarter held jobs.

Ben and Jen quizzed Change Please about its business model and drafted a plan to emulate it in France. Their first pitch was to a group of friends. Xav, who had recently quit his job and was looking to do something more meaningful, jumped at the opportunity to be involved. Together, the three began to unveil their barista training scheme, armed with information from Change Please.

Across the Channel, the documentation required was completely different and the entrepreneurs encountered obstacle after obstacle. They scouted around for similar social enterprises in France to see how they had made it work.

They came across another relative newcomer on the scene, Université du Café, a reintegration program that trains people serving prison sentences to become baristas so that they can find full-time employment upon release. Its slogan was "coffee that tastes like freedom." In 2019, the year of its inauguration, it trained four female detainees from Fleury-Mérogis Prison in the southern suburbs of Paris.

"There are no prerequisites," says Juliette Viard-Gaudin, Project Coordinator at Université du Café. "Just motivation and the curiosity to learn something new."

Université du Café had hoped to roll out its training program much more rapidly, but when Covid-19 pandemic hit in early 2020, training ground to a halt. It was a major impediment to Le

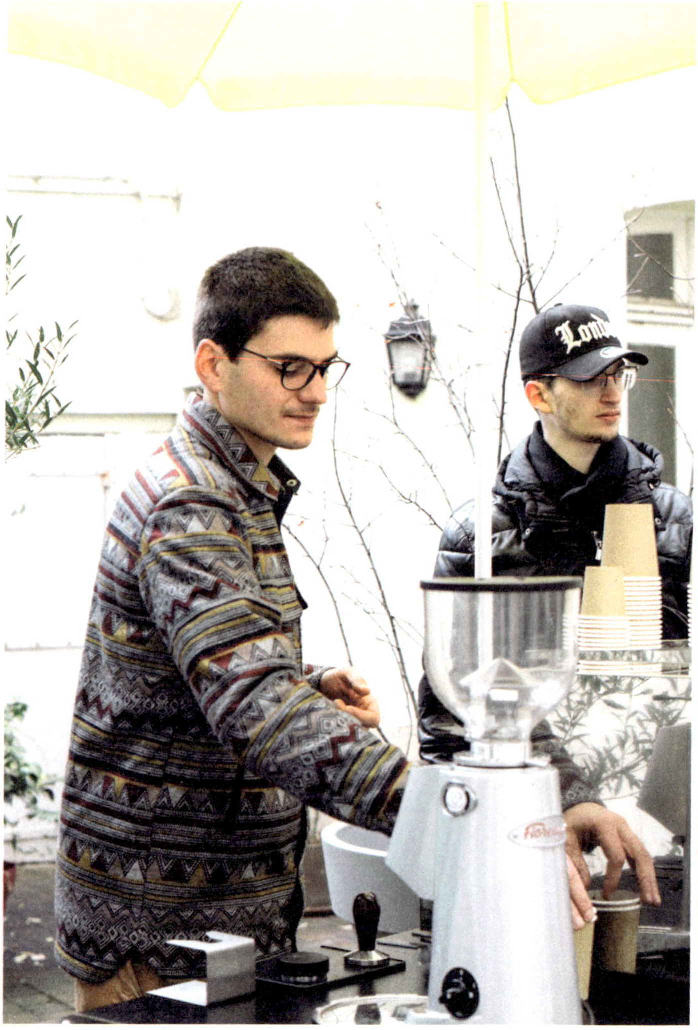

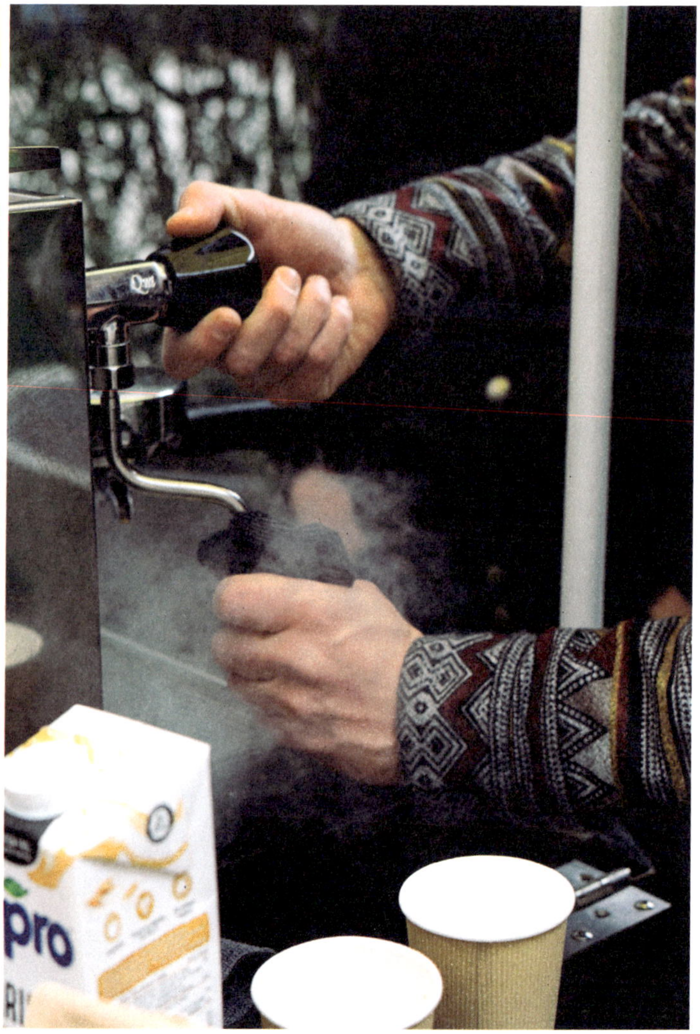
pro

PARIS — 155

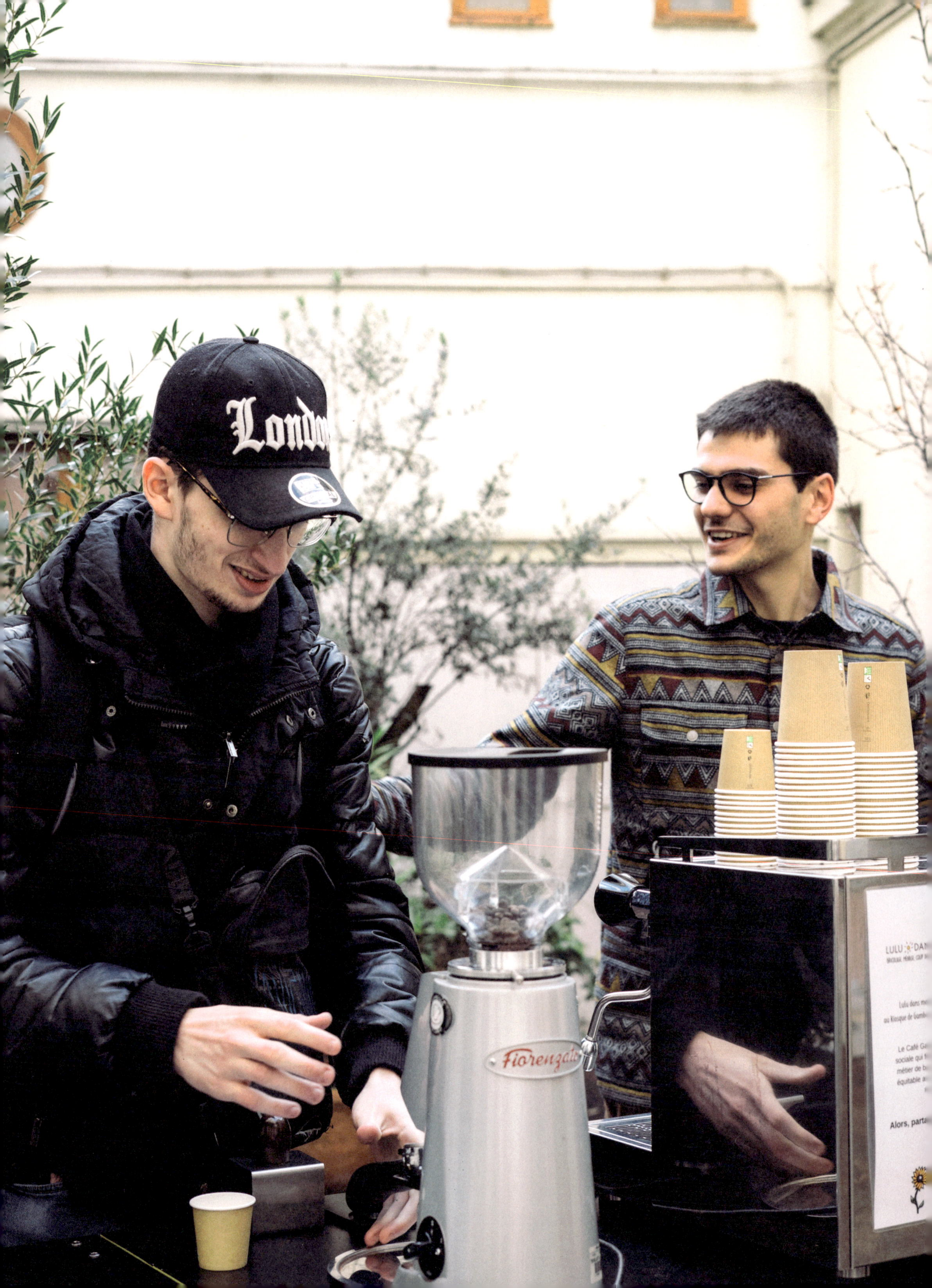

Café Gagnant's plans, too. Now, with the easing of restrictions, and armed with knowledge from Change Please and Université du Café, Le Café Gagnant has just finished training its first *stagiaire* (student trainee).

David, who is 22, is enrolled at the local art school, studying how to create video games, so he isn't typical of Le Café Gagnant's future protégés. This is, however, his first job and he had been struggling to find employment for some time. Through training David, the team has been able to understand exactly how long the training process is likely to take and the complications that could arise, before implementing it with others.

Le Café Gagnant will act as the final stage in a multi-layered reintegration process for people on the streets. In the first step, social workers will liaise directly with people on the streets of Paris to find those who are interested in participating in the program. This is followed by workshops, which can last anywhere from a week to a year, depending on the field of work and level of motivation. Le Café Gagnant is the final stage before full-time employment. In addition to teaching barista skills, Ben, Jen, and Xav are committed to supporting their trainees in the job hunt process too.

"Mondays are our training days," says David, explaining how his own work experience has taken place. "I learn the methods of how to make different drinks, then for the rest of the week I put it into practice."

"I think that it's a great idea, and I believe that anyone can learn to make good coffee with practice," he enthuses. "The trickiest part isn't learning to be a barista, it's customer service, and you have to be very positive every day. That's something that's harder to learn if you don't have good people skills, or if you're lacking in energy."

If anything is set to make Le Café Gagnant a success, it's its winning combination of the founders' motivations. They each had different reasons for being part of Le Café Gagnant. Ben was focused on helping people to reintegrate into society, and giving someone another chance. Jen loved the beauty of the whole procedure, and the idea that they could change lives through kindness and a cup of coffee. She's the artist of the team too, and its vibrant yellow tricycle was her design. For Xav, the key motivation was changing consumer habits. He wants people to appreciate the quality of the coffee that they're supplying, and the journey that both the bean and the barista have taken to supply a winning brew.

"At the moment, the biggest hurdle facing Le Café Gagnant is to find a permanent location. For now the baristas are restricted to serving coffee from [the] tricycle, and getting permits to do even that from the various Parisian *arrondissements* is a constant challenge."

"There's a lot of misunderstanding," says Xav. "People assume that we're working with ex-convicts and they complain that they don't want people with a criminal record coming to their area to serve coffee. But this isn't the case at all. They're confusing reintegration programs with rehabilitation, and many of the people that we work with [have never] had a criminal record."

Xav would like to open a proper coffee shop from which to operate, but cost is prohibitive.

"It would really simplify things!" he smiles. "We're so dependent on the weather at the moment too. On days like this, as you can imagine, we don't sell a lot of coffee."

While the process hasn't been as easy as the team at Le Café Gagnant had hoped, the founders are determined to make things work. To help speed up the roll-out, they've decided to merge with Change Please and use their combined knowledge and enthusiasm to help Parisians in need. As the rain intensifies, we break for shelter and David heads back to class. I'm convinced that Le Café Gagnant—or Change Please Paris as they'll soon become—will brew up winning change.

—

APPENDIX

Paris:

Atelier P1
157 Rue Marcadet, 75018
Paris, France

Back in Black
25 Rue Amelot, 75011
Paris, France

Belleville Brûlerie
14b Rue Lally-Tollendal, 75019
Paris, France

Boot Café
19 Rue du Pont aux Choux, 75003
Paris, France

Café de Flore
172 Bd Saint-Germain, 75006
Paris, France

Café Kitsuné Louvre
2 Pl. André Malraux, 75001
Paris, France

Café Kitsuné Palais Royal
51 Gal de Montpensier, 75001
Paris, France

Café Kitsuné Tuileries
208 Rue de Rivoli, 75001
Paris, France

Café Kitsuné Vertbois
30 Rue du Vertbois, 75003
Paris, France

Café Loustic
40 Rue Chapon, 75003
Paris, France

Café Mericourt
22 Rue de la Folie Méricourt, 75011
Paris, France

Café Nuances
25 Rue Danielle Casanova, 75001
Paris, France

Café Procope
13 Rue de l'Ancienne Comédie, 75006
Paris, France

Chanceux
57 Rue Saint-Maur, 75011
Paris, France

Charbon Café
109 Rue Oberkampf, 75011
Paris, France

Clove Coffee Shop
14 Rue Chappe, 75018
Paris, France

Coutume
47 Rue de Babylone, 75007
Paris, France

Coutume Fondation Fiminco
43 Rue de la Commune de Paris, 93230
Romainville, France

Dose
73 Rue Mouffetard, 75005
Paris, France

Dose
82 Place du Dr Félix Lobligeois, 75017
Paris, France

Dreamin' Man
140 Rue Amelot, 75011
Paris, France

Fringe
106 Rue de Turenne, 75003
Paris, France

Grand Café Tortoni
45 Rue de Saintonge, 75003
Paris, France

Herboristerie d'Hippocrate
42 Rue Saint-André des Arts, 75006
Paris, France

Herboristerie de la Place Clichy
87 Rue d'Amsterdam, 75008
Paris, France

Hexagone Café
121 Rue du Château, 75014
Paris, France

Holybelly Café
5 Rue Lucien Sampaix, 75010
Paris, France

I.O Café
16 Rue Dupetit-Thouars, 75003
Paris, France

Kawa
96 Rue des Archives, 75003
Paris, France

KB Caféshop
53 Av. Trudaine, 75009
Paris, France

La Caféothèque
52 Rue de l'Hôtel de ville, 75004
Paris, France

La Main Noire
12 Rue Cavallotti, 75018
Paris, France

La Palette
43 Rue de Seine, 75006
Paris, France

Les Deux Magots
6 Pl. Saint-Germain des Prés, 75006
Paris, France

Lomi
3 ter Rue Marcadet, 75018
Paris, France

Merci
111 Bd Beaumarchais, 75003
Paris, France

Motors Coffee
7 Rue des Halles, 75001
Paris, France

Noir Coffee Shop & Torréfacteur
120 Bd Haussmann, 75008
Paris, France

Noir Coffee Shops & Torréfacteur
9 Rue de Luynes, 75007
Paris, France

Nuance Café
16 Rue Linné, 75005
Paris, France

Officine Universelle Buly
45 rue de Saintonge, 75003
Paris, France

On Partage
137 bis Rue de Charonne, 75011
Paris, France

Poilâne
8 Rue du Cherche-Midi, 75006
Paris, France

Sain Boulangerie
15 Rue Marie et Louise, 75010
Paris, France

Saint Pearl
38 Rue des Saints-Pères, 75007
Paris, France

GLOSSARY

Strada Café
24 Rue Monge, 75005
Paris, France

Strada Café
94 Rue du Temple, 75003
Paris, France

Substance Café
30 Rue Dussoubs, 75002
Paris, France

Téléscope Café
5 Rue Villédo, 75001
Paris, France

Ten Belles - Paris 6
53 Rue du Cherche-Midi, 75006
Paris, France

Ten Belles - Paris 10
10 Rue de la Grange aux Belles, 75010
Paris, France

Ten Belles - Paris 17
17-19 Rue Breguet, 75011
Paris, France

Terres de Café
14 Rue Rambuteau, 75004
Paris, France

The Beans on Fire
7 Rue du Général Blaise, 75011
Paris, France

The Broken Arm
12 Rue Perrée, 75003
Paris, France

The Dancing Goat
117 Av. Gambetta, 75020
Paris, France

Toraya
10 Rue Saint-Florentin, 75001
Paris, France

Typica
8 Rue des Filles du Calvaire, 75003
Paris, France

**
This list represents coffee shops visited, referenced, or interviewed on background for the making of Drift, Volume 12: Paris.

Outside Paris:

Café du Monde
1039 Decatur St, 70116,
New Orleans, LA, United States

Fuglen
Universitetsgata 2, 0164
Oslo, Norway

La Cabra
Graven 20, 8000
Århus, Denmark

Arrondissement
Paris is divided into 20 districts, or *arrondissements*. These are often shortened to 1er (*premier*, "the first"), or 2eme through 20eme (*deuxième*, "the second," through *vingtième*, "twentieth").

Assemblage
The blending of coffee beans.

Café
While it means coffee, in France, it usually refers to a simple espresso.

Café allongé
Translates to "elongated coffee," as the espresso is stretched by adding hot water.

Café au lait
Coffee or espresso with a bit of hot or steamed milk added, usually made at home.

Café crème
Coffee or espresso drink with a bit of hot or steamed milk added, more commonly seen on menus.

Café décafeiné
Decaffeinated coffee.

Café minute
Coffee made-to-order.

Café serré
Is a "short shot" of a more highly concentrated espresso. Also known elsewhere as a ristretto.

L'art de vivre
The art of living.

Le Rive Gauche and Le Rive Droite
Paris is bisected by the Seine River, which flows east to west. Le Rive Gauche, or Left Bank, refers to the southern bank, while Rive Droite, or the Right Bank, refers to the northern bank.

Noisette
While it means "hazelnut" in French, the coffee drink *la noisette* is the equivalent of a *caffe macchiato*—espresso with a splash of milk, giving it the color of hazelnuts.

Quartier
A district, or neighborhood.

Torréfacteur
Someone who roasts coffee, or someone who sells roasted coffee.

PARIS

INSTAGRAM
@driftmag

TWITTER
@driftny

FACEBOOK
/driftny

WEBSITE
www.driftmag.com